THE LIVERPOOL LIFEBOAT DISASTER 1892

One man's search for a missing piece of history

Jim Sullivan

Published by:-
Avid Publications, Garth Boulevard
Bebington, Wirral, Merseyside.
CH63 5LS
Telephone / Fax: (44) 0151 645 2047
e-mail info @ AvidPublications.co.uk
website http//www.AvidPublications.co.uk

THE LIVERPOOL LIFEBOAT DISASTER 1892
by Jim Sullivan
ISBN 1 902964 10 1
© Jim Sullivan 2001
A CIP record for this book is available from the British Library

The right of James Sullivan to be identified as the Author of this work has been
asserted by him in accordance with the Copyright, Designs and Patent Act, 1993.

**Edited, typeset and cover design © William David Roberts MA, Avid
Publications 2001.**

**Cover painting: from an original by Tony Sullivan, the author's
brother.**

Printed and Bound by MFP Design & Print, Stretford, Manchester.

'Storm in the Mersey' by S.Walters

Acknowledgements

This book would simply never have happened without the assistance, encouragement and support of many, many people along the way.

I should like to put on record my special thanks to Miss Margaret Evans of the Records Department, Liverpool Maritime Museum.

Captain Roy Williams, M.D.& H.C.

Mr. Jeff Morris, honorary archivist of the Lifeboat Enthusiasts' Society.

Captain Brian McShane, M.D.& H.C.

Mr Anthony Hanney - Secretary Liverpool Branch RNLI

Mr Bev Brown, Ex- Coxswain, New Brighton Lifeboats

Also particular thanks are due to Mr & Mrs John and Pam Francis, respectively Secretary and Assistant Secretary of the Lifeboat Enthusiasts' Society.

WHAT THEY SAID ABOUT *THE LIVERPOOL LIFEBOAT DISASTER 1892:* -

'...charting a remarkable *'last journey'* for everyone involved in the Liverpool Lifeboat Disaster of 1892... this book is clearly a labour of love...but it is far more than that... It is a story that deserves to be told, and you have told it with amazing commitment and clarity.'

Alan Bleasdale

'... a most readable and detailed account of a part of Lifeboat history about which very little was known before...unravels a forgotten part of Liverpool's maritime history.'

Jeff Morris - Honorary Archivist - Lifeboat Enthusiasts Society

'... having served in the very waters in which these events took place... the book captures the atmosphere and sets the scenes admirably. The Liverpool Lifeboat Disaster will make a notable addition to the history of our great port and will highlight some of the effort and sacrifice that went into building it.'

Capt. Roy Williams - Master Mariner

' An engrossing read... a MUST for anyone with even the slightest interest in nautical aspects of Merseyside History. An extremely valuable document for the City of Liverpool.... encapsulates this seafaring drama with great humanity and precision.'

Brian Jacques - BBC Radio Merseyside

' Fascinating social history...a tribute to those men who lost their lives in the great storm at sea.'

Gary Bleasdale -- Actor & playwright

'Extremely well researched, written and presented...this most valuable document is an integral part of Liverpool's maritime history and culture.'

Tony Furlong and Jim Power - Liverpool playwrights

To the memory of all
Lifeboat personnel, both
past and present, thank you
all. You are indeed a special
breed of people.

To my dear wife Eileen,
thank you for always
waiting for me.

And to my mother,
Catherine, for sharing her
wonderful memories with
me.

The Author

Jim Sullivan was born and bred in Liverpool and joined the Royal Navy in 1956.
During his time in the RN he served aboard Britain's last battleship, HMS *Vanguard* and also the country's first guided missile Destroyer, HMS *Devonshire*. Jim joined her on completion in 1962 at Cammell Laird's shipyard Birkenhead, where she was built and also where his father, a Ship's Plater, had worked on her construction. On a courtesy visit to the United States, the Captain and ship's company of *Devonshire*, Jim included, were given the honour of being made Freemen of the City of Philadelphia on October 11th 1963. He also spent part of his time in 'the senior service' as an official guide aboard Nelson's flagship, HMS *Victory*.
On completion of his Navy service he joined the Merchant Navy were he served in ocean going rescue tugs and other vessels.
In 1970 he joined the Pilotage division of the Mersey Docks and Harbour Board serving seven years on Pilot launches before transferring to the Dredging department where he is still a seaman aboard the *Mersey Venture*.
Whilst working in the Pilot Service Jim was awarded the Bronze Medal of the Liverpool Shipwreck and Humane Society for his bravery in rescuing a young woman from the River Mersey in December 1973.
He began to research the story of the Liverpool Lifeboat Disaster after recalling stories he had heard as a child from older members of his seafaring family, in particular his mother Catherine.
Jim is married to Eileen and they have five children. He still lives in Liverpool today.

Yet lovely is the sight

When stranger though he be to the distressed

A good man gives assistance

Chapter One

An Old Story

Ever since I can remember, and especially after I had decided to make the sea my calling in 1956, I had heard tales related by members of my family, in particular my mother, of a lifeboat tragedy off the Port of Liverpool that had claimed the life of my great grandfather, Emmanuel Rodriguez. At the time the stories meant little to me, and I duly went away to sea, first in the Royal Navy and then the Merchant Navy.

In 1969 I left the deep sea and together with my dear wife Eileen and our young family moved from Plymouth - her home town - to my home town of Liverpool where I had managed to get a job with the Mersey Docks and Harbour Board as an able-seaman in the wreck crew. Shortly after joining them I was offered a job aboard Hoveringham's new dredger *Hoveringham IV* (building at Appledore, North Devon) which I accepted, joining her on 5 May 1969 as bosun.

At about the same time my uncle Tony, a fireman in the Merchant Navy, was retired from the sea on health grounds.

Tony and I got together regularly after this, and over a pint our conversation invariably turned to the sea and ships. During the course of one such conversation the subject of the lifeboat tragedy came up. I asked what he knew of the story and to my surprise found that he knew as little as I did, and what he did know differed greatly to the stories I had been told over the years.

It was then we decided to try and find the facts behind the true story. This proved to be no easy matter; we had so little reliable information to go on, and absolutely no idea how to research such things. The only thing we did know for certain was that Tony's grandfather - my great grandfather - had been lost at sea in a lifeboat disaster somewhere in the Mersey Estuary, possibly in the last quarter of the nineteenth century and (according to the stories) his body had been recovered on Crosby foreshore some ten days after the tragedy and was thought to be buried in Ford cemetery, Liverpool. This information had been given to us by my mother (Tony's sister) but no member of our family could furnish us with any positive facts. Those that may have been able to were now long dead.

No documents belonging to my great grandparents had survived, no birth or death certificates, no marriage licence, not even a photograph; and so the search began.

Armed with our limited information we first paid a visit to Ford cemetery, hoping we might find great grandfather's grave, if indeed he was buried there, but after several visits we had found no trace. The records office at Ford lodge could not help us either unless we could provide them with a date, or at least the year of the interment.

We next tried the local maritime history department at the

Brown-Picton and Hornby libraries in Liverpool. Here we checked on lifeboat disasters around the Lancashire coast during the latter part of the last century; again nothing. But having no dates or names to go on, not even the name or station of the lifeboat in which great grandfather had served, this result was hardly surprising.

We did, however, gain one small piece of information; there had been two great storms in the latter part of the last century, one in the 1870s and another in the 1890s. Both storms were severely felt in the Mersey Estuary and the Irish Sea. Not much, but every little helps. At least it was something we could check on.

After spending six months with Hoveringham's I was laid off in November 1969. There not being many jobs for seamen locally I decided to go back to sea after the Christmas holiday. In the meantime Tony and I turned our attention to the old newspapers kept in the micro film unit of the Brown-Picton and Hornby libraries. We started with the first edition of the *Liverpool Echo* for January 1870. We visited the libraries many times in the weeks that followed. Going through the newspapers page by page proved to be a long, slow task and by Christmas we had found nothing relating to the Liverpool lifeboat disaster.

With the new year I was ready to go back to sea, having had my Merchant Navy records transferred from Plymouth to Liverpool, necessary to enable me to ship out of Liverpool. All I needed was a ship, and the research into the mystery surrounding the death of Emmanuel Rodriguez would be left with Tony.

Then out of the blue, on the morning of 21 January 1970, I received a telegram from the Pilotage Division of the Mersey Docks and Harbour Board, offering me a job. After an interview with Captain Whiteside, Assistant Superintendent of Pilotage at the old Pilotage office, Canning Dock (now part of the Liverpool Maritime Museum) I was taken on. During my previous brief time with the MDHB I had applied for a job in the Pilot launches when a vacancy had arisen, but had been unsuccessful. Fortunately however, my name had been kept on the list and now the job I had wanted so much in the past was mine, and I would not have to go back to deep sea work to earn my living.

All through 1970, whenever we got the chance, Tony and I would continue the search through the old newspapers. By Christmas 1970 we had still found nothing of interest to us, having covered the whole of the 1870s and most of the 1880s. Then on Boxing Day 1970 Tony took ill and died eleven days later, aged 46 years. With Tony's passing I lost interest in researching the story.

I remained with the Liverpool Pilotage service for seven years before transferring to the Dredging department, joining the Grab Hopper Dredger *Mersey Compass* in 1977. In May 1983 I joined the dock company's new Trailer Suction Dredger *Mersey Venture*. Most of her work is done out in the Mersey Estuary, dredging in the two main deep water channels leading from seaward into the port of Liverpool. She has two crews, who work a week away aboard the *Venture* and a week at home. Out there in the Mersey Estuary when the visibility is good you can see the Cumbrian coastline to the north and as far as the Ormes Head, Llandudno, in the south west. And when it started to blow, especially from the north west and I saw the waves crashing across the sandbanks and washing over the lonely wreck of the *Pegu[1]*, with her one remaining mast pointing sadly towards the sky, then rushing on to thunder against the shore, I would get to thinking .... that somewhere out in this great bay many years ago a lifeboat drama had been acted out in which my great grand father lost his life. Then I would recall the hours Tony and I had spent trying to discover the story surrounding that drama.

One night in October 1986 I read an article in a magazine about the wreck of the German barque *Mexico*. The *Mexico* was on passage from Liverpool to Guayaquil, Ecuador when she was driven ashore and wrecked in the Ribble Estuary on the 9th December 1886. Three lifeboats were launched to her assistance, crewed by 44 men. That night 27 lifeboatmen lost their lives.

4

S.S. Pegu

Liverpool Landing Stage, 1889. TSS Majestic coming alongside.

Was my great grandfather among them? Once again I became curious to know the story of this lifeboat tragedy, and became determined to find out.

First I wrote to the Maritime History Department of the Picton Library, telling them *my* story and explaining the different avenues that had been explored. In reply, Dr. Alan Scarth noted two incidents that could possibly have a bearing on the subject. The first, in 1875 involved the Liverpool No. 1 lifeboat that was badly damaged trying to save the crew of the American ship *Ellen Southerd*, aground in Crosby Channel [2.] The Liverpool lifeboat, with great difficulty, managed to get alongside the stricken ship and took off the crew, including the captain and his wife. On casting off, the coxswain ordered the foresail to be set but before this could be done a huge wave struck the lifeboat on the quarter, filling the partly set foresail and capsizing her, throwing all 32 on board into the sea. The New Brighton lifeboat ' *Willie and Arthur* ' then came up and working through the wreckage, got alongside the upturned hull of the Liverpool boat and picked up 20 persons, 8 of the *Ellen Southerd* ' crew and 12 lifeboatmen, one of whom died minutes later. Two lifeboatmen were drowned, as were the captain, his wife and 7 crew of the *Ellen Southerd* '. None of the lifeboatmen lost was my great grandfather.

The second incident, in 1884, involved the New Brighton lifeboat *Stuart Hey*, she being virtually wrecked attempting to rescue the crew of the Liverpool ship *Juno* bound for Calcutta with a cargo of salt. The *Juno* had gone aground on Taylor's Bank; due to the severity of the weather the New Brighton boat found it impossible to get alongside, so the *Stuart Hey* stood by the grounded *Juno* for 10 hours, waiting for a moderation in the weather. During that time she made three unsuccessful attempts to get alongside. Sighting the Liverpool lifeboat coming up, the New Brighton crew, now utterly exhausted, proceeded back to their station. The Liverpool crew watched the progress of the *Stuart Hey* and at one point thought she had been overwhelmed by an exceptional sea. Upon reaching the spot where the Liverpool men expected to find the New Brighton boat wrecked, they caught sight of her still heading for home under a scrap of sail.

The Liverpool lifeboat, on trying to return to the *Juno*, received a severe buffeting, but eventually managed to get alongside the Formby Lightship, where a hawser was passed and they hung on in sight of the *Juno* and waited, as the New Brighton men had, for a lull in the storm. But the lull never came and as the storm raged on the *Juno*'s masts fell one by one, then she began to break up and suddenly collapsed beneath the waves.

The Liverpool lifeboat at once cast off and began to search for survivors in that terrible sea, but none were found, all hands from the *Juno* being lost. There was no loss of life from either lifeboat that night. Once again I had no answers to my questions.

One day, while discussing the subject with my mother, she told me that she thought the name of the lifeboat great grandfather had served in was the *Maxwell*. She said she seemed to remember that name being mentioned by her mother. With that, I wrote to the Royal National Lifeboat Institution, asking if any of the lifeboats that had taken part in the rescue attempt to the *Mexico* had borne the name *Maxwell* and if the name Emmanuel Rodriguez appeared on the list of lifeboatmen lost that night. Their reply gave me the first piece of information that eventually enabled me to unfold the full story of the Liverpool lifeboat disaster.

Mr. Tony Instrall of the RNLI told me that no information concerning the loss of my great grandfather could be found in their records; that the name *Maxwell* had never been borne by any Institution lifeboat but there *had been* a full rigged sailing ship of that, name. Mr. Instrall also sent me a copy of a page taken from the Lifeboat Journal for the year 1893. A small paragraph told of a rescue attempt by the New Brighton lifeboat *Henry Richardson* and one of the Liverpool lifeboats, to the full rigged sailing ship *Maxwell*. The attempted rescue had cost three Liverpool lifeboatmen their lives; the date, July 19th, 1892. The report gave a brief account of the rescue attempt, but did not give the names of the men lost, or the name of the lifeboat.

But now at last I felt sure I was on the right course - and so I was. What I could not understand, with such loss of life from the Liverpool lifeboat, was how the RNLI who keep such detailed records of their activities and services, had no record of the names of the victims of the disaster. The reason for this soon became clear. When first reading the brief report on the rescue attempt to the *Maxwell* I had overlooked one very important point, for it stated that the Liverpool lifeboat that had put off to aid the *Maxwell* belonged to the Mersey Docks & Harbour Board. This was the reason why the RNLI had no details of the lifeboats

I had always assumed that all lifeboat stations around the British Isles were under the control of the RNLI, but this had not always been the case. The Mersey Docks & Harbour Board, (MDHB, as it was until 1972 when it became a Company) was, by an Act of Parliament, bound to provide a lifeboat service covering the Mersey Estuary. This was so until 1894 when after a number of meetings between the MDHB and the RNLI it was agreed that the former would hand over control of its lifeboat stations to the RNLI.

It was agreed that the MDHB would donate an annual sum of money to the RNLI, also that of the five lifeboat stations belonging to and under the control of the MDHB (Point of Ayr, Hoylake, Hilbre Island Magazines, Liverpool and Formby) the one at Liverpool landing stage would be abolished. Thus on the 1st July 1894 the MDHB handed control of its lifeboat service to the RNLI.

Since the RNLI had no record of my great grandfather there was a good possibility that he had been employed as a lifeboatman by the MDHB - the very same establishment that I am employed by.What a strange coincidence if he had.

At about the time I had asked for help with my research from the Picton library, I had been in telephone contact with Mr. Bev

Brown, ex coxswain of the New Brighton lifeboat. In a very long and informative written reply to my many questions, Mr. Brown confirmed the service to the *Maxwell* by the New Brighton and Liverpool lifeboats in July 1892, also informing me that the Liverpool lifeboat was the No. 2 boat (the MDHB did not give names to any of their lifeboats, only numbers) and that he had no details of the men lost from her.

Mr. Brown went on to tell me that all records covering the Liverpool lifeboat service had been destroyed when the Dock Board building was bombed and set on fire during the last war. It now seemed that my only hope lay in old newspapers or other documents not directly associated with the Liverpool lifeboat service.

I next went to see Captain Roy Williams, the MDHB Safety Officer, at his office in the Dock Company building on Liverpool pierhead. I had known Roy for some time from his days as a relieving Master in the MDHB dredgers. I explained to him what I was about and his response proved to be very helpful. I next requested access to the MDHB archives, only to be informed that they had recently been removed from the Dock building and divided into two separate groups. One group was housed in the new Maritime Museum at the Albert Dock, the other in the Liverpool Maritime Archives Department, Islington, Liverpool. At the time both departments were in some disarray, being quite new establishments. With so much newly acquired material to sort out, it would be some little time before any real research could be conducted there.

In the meantime Roy Williams had been busy on my behalf. First he had managed to get a photocopy of an entry made in the Dock Board Wreck Book for July 1892, which once again confirmed that the Liverpool lifeboat had lost three men, but again no names were given. Now it was time to go back to the old newspapers.

Roy Williams was already doing research work of his own at

the Picton Library, and offered to check the newspapers for July 1892.

In the meantime I had been busy at the Liverpool Maritime Museum, but could find no reference to the Liverpool lifeboats in the museum's archives. I did however, get details of the sailing ship *Maxwell*.

On 25 November 1986 I received a message from Roy Williams telling me that he had found articles in the *Liverpool Echo* referring to the Liverpool lifeboat disaster of July 1892. He informed me that the print was very small and difficult to read and that good reading glasses or a magnifying glass would be required. He had very kindly ordered photocopies to be forwarded to me. I did not wait to receive them but went straight to the Picton Library microfilm unit, and there at long last laid out before me was what I had been searching for.

In the *Liverpool Echo* dated Wednesday 20th July 1892 was a report relating to a great storm and the tragedy that had befallen the Liverpool lifeboat which had resulted in the loss of three lifeboatmen, one of them being named as Emmanuel Rodriguez. At last I knew for certain that my great grandfather had indeed been a lifeboatman who had lost his life at sea while attempting to save the lives of others.

Now the real search for information was to begin. To me the newspaper report was only the beginning of the story, I wanted to know the whole of it.

This was to prove no easy task and would take another two years to uncover, helped and encouraged along the way by many people whom I cannot thank enough.

This is the story as I found it.

Notes: -

1. S.S. *Pegu* was built in 1921 by W. Denny & Co. of Dumbarton for the British & Burma Steam Navigation Co., owners Mr. P. Henderson & Son Ltd. A passenger-cargo ship of 8,183 tons, steel screw, she had a series of mishaps during her service: damaged by bunker fire whilst loading at Rangoon, 1922, collided with the moored Italian S.S. *Isco* leaving Marseilles, June 1928 (little damage), capsized the tug *Toxteth* which was assisting her out of Brunswick Dock, Liverpool on 27 Jan. 1937 with the loss of 5 lives, outward bound from Liverpool to Glasgow for Burma 25 Nov. 1939 stranded on Taylor's Bank in the Mersey Estuary and became a total loss. All 103 passengers and crew were taken off by the New Brighton lifeboat. Her foremast remained standing until March 1987 when the tug *'Wallasey'*, disabled in a storm, collided with the mast, bringing it down. (see photograph page 5)

2. The Liverpool No. 1 Tubular lifeboat launched to the assistance of the American ship *Ellen Southerd* 27 September 1875.

Crew members: Coxswain James Martin, James Conley, Charles Dangelow, William Steward, George Lee, William Gregory, William Ruffler, James Munday, Hugh Beard, John Dolmar, Samuel Richards, John Boyle, Robert Moore (died), James Yates (died) plus one other, unnamed.

Coxswain R.J. Thomas of the New Brighton lifeboat *Willie & Arthur* was awarded a gold medal by the American Government for his efforts that night.

Extract from Mersey Docks & Harbour Board Wreck Book, 1892

Chapter Two

The Sailing of the Maxwell

At 2.30 on the morning of July 19th 1892, a message was received at the New Brighton lifeboat station, that a vessel had been sighted showing distress signals.

The New Brighton lifeboat *Henry Richardson* (coxswain William Martin) was quickly manned by her crew of 16, and slipping her moorings was taken in tow by the steam paddle tug *Brilliant Star* (owned by Mr. Harry Strong of the Brilliant Star Steam Tug Co. of Liverpool.)

In heavy seas and with a full northwesterly gale blowing, the *Brilliant Star* proceeded out towards Formby Channel where they found the three masted schooner *Renown* ashore at Formby Hole, near to Formby lifeboat house.[1]

When the lifeboat arrived the tug *Hercules* was standing by the *Renown* preparing to take her in tow. Three of the lifeboatmen boarded the stranded schooner and helped to secure a towline from the *Hercules*, they then assisted the schooner's crew in raising her anchor. This being achieved, the *Renown* was hauled off the shore by the tug and towed into Liverpool and safety.

The "Grace Harwar", sister ship to the "Maxwell". Seen here at sea under sail 1889.

The New Brighton lifeboat, having recovered her three crewmen, and her services no longer being required, returned to her station. The lifeboat men`s respite was not to last long.

At the time these events were taking place the sailing ship *Maxwell* was making final preparations for sea in Birkenhead Docks, across the river from Liverpool. The *Maxwell*, a fine full rigged iron built sailing ship of 1,800 tons had arrived in her home port of Liverpool some weeks earlier in ballast from Dunkirk. Her previous voyage had taken her from Greenhithe on the Kent coast around Cape Horn to San Francisco, California.

Group photograph on the main deck of "Grace Harwar" 1889.

Upon discharging her cargo in San Francisco she was ordered to proceed along the west coast of America to Astoria, Oregon, to load wheat for Europe. On her arrival off the Columbia river she was delayed for three days as the bar was impassable. During this time the *Maxwell* was in collision with the ship *Kirkcudbrightshire*' but sustained only slight damage and her crew carried out temporary repairs.

The morning after the collision the *Maxwell* crossed the bar, assisted by a tug and Pilot, and anchored off Astoria to await loading. While at anchor she was caught in a sudden squall and the windlass was torn from its bed, resulting in the loss of the anchor and cable, the *Maxwell* being very nearly driven ashore.

After the squall, the ship's Master, Captain T.G. Fraser of Liskeard, hired a barge with a powerful windlass. After two days of toil the *Maxwell*'s crew had managed to recover the anchor and cable, and also to get one side of her windlass in working order, but on close examination they found that the windlass bed plate had been cracked when the windlass had carried away. Following this discovery Captain Fraser made arrangements to have the *Maxwell* towed to Portland to effect repairs.

Now with the damage sustained in the collision with the 'Kirkcudbrightshire' temporarily repaired, a new bed plate for the windlass cast and fitted, and the windlass restored to full working order, the *Maxwell* returned to Astoria where she went alongside and loaded with grain. This completed, she set sail for Queenstown, Ireland, the passage taking 102 days.

On her arrival at Queenstown Captain Fraser was ordered to proceed to Dunkirk, where the cargo was quickly discharged; *Maxwell* then left under tow for Liverpool. On arrival in the Mersey Captain Fraser could not acquire the services of a stern tug, and whilst docking in a squall the ship's head was driven against the pier head, increasing the damage caused off Astoria.

The *Maxwell* was dry docked in Liverpool and repairs to her damaged bow plates were carried out. After this she was moved across river to Birkenhead for loading with coal for San Francisco. This completed, her crew set about making ready for sea. The *Maxwell* carried 29 crew all told, including 4 apprentices. 19 of the men, including Mr R.G.Mowatt, the Mate, came from Liverpool.[2]

In the early hours of Tuesday morning the 19th July the *Maxwell* was once again ready for sea. With her Pilot embarked and her tugs in attendance the order was given to let go. At 5.30 am the last of her mooring ropes were slipped and the ship moved slowly away from her berth. Once clear of the dock system and out into the river Mersey, she was taken in tow by the steam paddle tug *Great Western* (Owned by W.L. Thomas Jolliff of Liverpool), to begin the long haul out past the north west light ship to the open sea where she would cast off her tug. The weather that third week of July 1892 bore no resemblance to summer. For some days prior to the *Maxwell's* sailing, gales had ravaged the British Isles, accompanied by deluges of rain and very low temperatures. The gales had been severely felt in the Irish Sea and the Mersey

How the Maxwell would have appeared leaving the port of Liverpool, July 1892.

The Liverpool Pilot Cutter George Holt.. Courtesy of Captain Roberts, Liverpool Pilotage.

Estuary, causing a great deal of damage to the channel, with winds gusting up to hurricane force and veering from west northwest to north easterly.

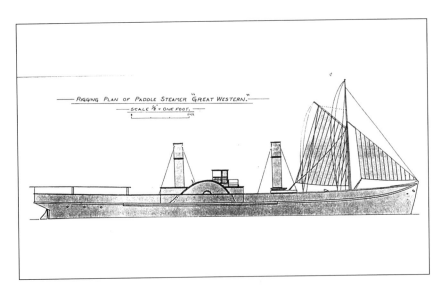

The steam paddle tug "Great Western". The "Great Western" and her sister ship "Great Britain" were built by William Simons of Renfrew for the Liverpool fleet of W. & A. Jolliffe in 1876. They were 154.1 ft. x 23.7ft. x 12.7 ft. with a gross tonnage of 300 tons. The "Great Western" was the tug that towed the sailing ship "Maxwell" out to sea from Liverpool on July 19 1892.

And now on this summer morning, as the *Maxwell* was being coaxed along, aloof and magnificent, by the ever attentive bustling steam tug, the gale which had blown from the west northwest in the early hours, and had witnessed the saving of the schooner *Renown* had veered to the north and moderated to a strong breeze.

In this setting the tug and her charge proceeded slowly on their way, passing close to New Brighton where the *Henry Richardson* now lay at her moorings, then on out past the Crosby and Formby lightships towards the bar lightship.

Soon after passing the bar around noon, the Pilot Cutter was sighted. The Pilot, his duties complete, paid his respects to the *Maxwell* 's Master and boarded the Pilot Cutter's punt for the short journey across to the Pilot boat.[3]

Once the Pilot had been disembarked the Master of the *Great Western* set course for the NORTHWEST lightship *Star* which lay 8 miles west by north a half north (W by N½ N) of the bar lightship. During the slow haul from the Mersey bar to the north west lightship, the wind had gathered in strength and veered once more, this time to the north east. As the lightship drew abeam the wind had increased to gale force. The *Great Western* was by now having difficulty controlling the *Maxwell*, and tried zigzagging to hold her to the wind. To assist in this Captain Fraser ordered the lower staysails to be set, but as the crew unfurled each sail it was blown away. The wind had now reached storm force, with heavy seas starting to break over both tug boat and sailing ship. The Master of the *Great Western*, realising that the situation was becoming desperate, decided to return to Liverpool.

The decision made, the *Great Western* 's helm was eased slowly over to starboard, bringing both vessels around through the wind. The wind strength had now reached hurricane force and veered to the north northeast at times. The seas were running very high causing the *Maxwell* to plunge heavily, her decks continually awash; before the turn could be completed the hawser parted.

Now began a frantic race against time to secure a new tow line before the *Maxwell* was driven ashore by the fury of the storm. It was impossible to anchor in such tremendously big seas.

The *Maxwell* 's helm was kept hard over, with the mizzen yards backed and the fore -yards run square in an attempt to keep her bows to the wind and thus lessen the drift towards the unwelcome shore.

19

The Northwest Lightship 'Star' on Station 1885-1926.

*Built 1885 by R.J Evans & Co. of Liverpool for the Mersey Docks
and Harbour Board. She was built of iron and weighed 105 tons.
Stationed 8 miles to the northwest of the Bar lightship she marked the
outermost limits of the Mersey approaches.
When abeam of the northwest lightship, the great outward bound
sailing ships of the day, under tow of tugs, would cast off their tow here,
weather permitting , and set sail to begin their long voyages.
In November 1926 the Star was withdrawn and replaced by an
unmanned boat beacon. She then became a reserve lightship based at
Herculaneum Dock and used to replace the lightships at the Bar,
Formby and Crosby stations when these vessels came in for survey.
During the post war years she became a watch vessel used to mark
wrecks or other obstructions.
The Northwest lightship station was abolished in 1927.
The Star was broken up in the 1960s.
In the photograph above the Star is seen flying the signal 'Goodbye'
The photograph of the Star was taken by the late Mr. B. Fielden, a
local ship's photographer. Courtesy of Mr Craig. J.M. Carter.*

The hawser that had parted was the *Great Western*'s. The *Maxwell* had aboard a new 5-inch steel wire hawser which was quickly broken out, and after much hard work in appalling conditions, was passed through the towing pipe⁴ and laid out along the lee side to the quarter in readiness for the tug to pick up and continue the tow.

The tug's crew had in the meantime cleared away the broken hawser and her captain had manoeuvred his tug to the lee side of *Maxwell*. After a number of approaches and a few narrow escapes from collision, a heaving line was at last passed aboard the *Maxwell* a long length of 3 -inch manila rope was bent onto the heaving line, the Manilla being used as a messenger to haul the heavy wire hawser across to the tug. Once the hawser had been made fast aboard *Great Western* she proceeded to tow her charge back towards Liverpool, much to the relief of *Maxwell*'s crew, the tug being their only hope. In such narrow waters, with so many sandbanks, and a hurricane blowing which ruled out any attempt to set sail, the *Maxwell* was completely helpless.

No sooner had the tow been resumed than the tug found herself struggling once more to keep control of her charge. There had been no let up in the storm during this time, on the contrary in had grown in ferocity. The waves were now so big and violent that the *Great Western*, a paddle tug, was losing most of her power due to the sea throwing her paddles out of the water. Her Master tried zigzagging again, battling against wind and sea to keep control of the *Maxwell*. At one stage they were driven round so far as to get before the wind, causing the *Maxwell* to be pooped⁵ twice. Captain Fraser observed this was a thing she had never done in the open sea even in the heaviest of gales. At about 10 p.m. they passed close to the Bar lightship.

The tide was now ebbing with no change in the wind force or direction. Staying close to the buoys on their port side where the deepest water was to be found, they proceeded back across the Mersey bar, on which a massive sea was running.

All hands were hoping against hope that they would re-cross safely, when both vessels were lifted on the crest of a huge wave and as they sank in the trough the *Maxwell*'s crew felt her give an indescribable tremor. This happened several times, then she grounded with such force that spars were broken and the crew thrown to the deck.

Miraculously, nobody was injured and the towline held; *Great Western*, sticking bravely to her task, tried desperately to pull the stricken vessel off, but the sea had overwhelmed her, sweeping her decks from end to end. There was one final shudder and a great crash, the hawser parted and alone once again, the *Maxwell* settled on an even keel and all was quiet except for the roar of the elements.

The *Maxwell* had foundered on Little Burbo Bank, and sank about quarter of a mile westward of Q2 red buoy, her bows facing east south east. The tugmaster, realising that he could be of no further assistance, it being impossible to get alongside *Maxwell* to take off her crew, proceeded with all possible speed towards Liverpool for assistance, firing distress signals on the way.

The crew of the *Maxwell* tried to launch the ship's boats when she grounded, but so fierce was the storm and so big and powerful the waves, this proved to be an impossible task, some boats being smashed to pieces and the davits being carried away. The crew then mustered as far aft on the poop deck as they possibly could, and in that ink black night with the waves and spray lashing continuously over them and the wind screaming and tearing at them they expected every moment that their ship could break up beneath them, surrendering them to the merciless sea. So, in great fear for their lives the *Maxwell*'s crew clung to the rigging or whatever else they could, and prayed for deliverance from the tempest.

Shortly after the *Maxwell* had run aground and *Great Western* had departed on her mission of mercy, the inward bound schooner *Rambler* of Preston, proceeding under greatly reduced sail, saw the stranded *Maxwell* too late to take avoiding action. She struck the *Maxwell*`s port quarter with such force as to dismast herself, sustaining considerable damage, with most of her gear being carried away. *Maxwell*`s crew were helpless to assist and could only watch in horror as the '*Rambler*`, now no more than a tangled wreck, drifted away into the night, with the crew of the *Maxwell* believing that she would soon founder.

The schooner 'Rambler` [6].
*In the early hours of the morning July 20th 1892 the schooner Rambler of Preston inward for Liverpool and under greatly reduced sail due to the severity of the weather, collided with the stranded '*Maxwell*" with such force as to dismast herself.*

Notes:-

1. The "Renown", 127 tons and carrying a cargo of timber, belonged to Mr. A.C. Shaw of Runcorn.

2. The "Maxwell" was built in Liverpool in 1887 by the shipbuilders T.Royden & Sons for the Liverpool shipowners Johnson & Sproule whose offices were at No. 26 Old Hall Street, Liverpool. She had proved herself to be a well-designed and weatherly ship. She measured 269ft. x 39ft. x 23.5ft. and subsequently a sister ship the "Grace Harwar' was built in 1889 - broken up at Rosyth, 1935. (see photograph)

3. The Liverpool Pilotage Service employed a number of sailing pilot boats, mostly schooners (schooner-yachts) which kept station at the Bar to board or receive Pilots. They were phased out by the steam pilot boats from around 1896.

4. A rounded iron or steel pipe shaped aperture fitted right into the bows of the vessel atop the stem post. Also known as a fairlead but in the Royal Navy known as a Bullring.

5. A ship is pooped when a heavy sea breaks over her stern or quarter when she is running before the wind in a gale. The danger is being swung by the force of the wave broadside on to the sea. Small craft like yachts can be completely swamped and sunk by the volume of water coming aboard.

6. Built 1889 by Nicholson & Marsh at Glasson Dock Lancaster for J.Helme of Lancaster. Yard Number 84966. Cost £1663-5-0d. A two masted top-sail schooner of 83 tons she measured 84ft 4 inches x 19 ft 9 inches x 8ft 2 inches.

In 1901 she was acquired by M.Nicholson of Fleetwood and then by R.Gardner & Son. In 1925 she was fitted with a 4 cylinder paraffin engine. Her last entry in Lloyds Register of Shipping was in 1928.

Chapter Three

Lifeboats to the Rescue

A t approximately 11 o'clock that night the first signals of
distress were sighted on shore by the Formby lifeboat
station and by the New Brighton Coastguard. The
lookouts at both stations noted that the signals were being
discharged from the direction of the Little Burbo Bank, near to the
Mersey Bar.

Those in charge of the Formby lifeboat station immediately
summoned the lifeboat crew - the second time they had been
called out that day. With the minimum of delay the Formby
lifeboat was launched. It was impossible for her crew to set sail in
those conditions so Coxswain John Aindow ordered his crew to
man the oars and pull the lifeboat on the long and hazardous
ʳoyage out to the Bar some seven miles distant.

Meanwhile those in charge of the New Brighton Coastguard

station fired their own distress rockets indicating that a vessel was in difficulty in the vicinity of the Bar. The crew of the New Brighton lifeboat were at once summoned to their station. As with the Formby lifeboat, this was the second time their services had been called on that day.

Coxswain William Martin of the New Brighton lifeboat, upon reaching the lifeboat station shortly after 11.00 pm. set about firing other rockets in order to secure the services of a tug to tow the lifeboat out to sea (a luxury not afforded the Formby lifeboat) and also to alert the superintendent of the Liverpool lifeboats, stationed at the Prince's landing stage, to the fact that the Liverpool lifeboat was also required. It was common practice for the New Brighton and Liverpool lifeboats to work together once the call for assistance had gone out.

Mr. J. Brett, Assistant Secretary of the New Brighton lifeboat branch, had by now arrived at the lifeboat station (situated near to the New Brighton ferry) and, taking over from William Martin, he continued to fire red rockets while the lifeboat's crew manned their boat which was laying alongside the pier.

Once the crew had taken their places in the boat, the coxswain gave the order to cast off and the New Brighton lifeboat 'Henry Richardson' (then the largest of the Tubular lifeboats in service measuring 43ft. x 12ft.) moved away from the pier and lay a little way off with her 16 -man crew awaiting the arrival of a tug.

The glare from the distress rockets had started to attract an enormous crowd of people, who despite terrible weather conditions hurried up from all directions to New Brighton pier and promenade, and a scene of considerable expectation and excitement prevailed. At the George's landing stage at the Liverpool pierhead (approximately 3 miles up river of New Brighton and on the east bank) the stage master observed a rocket going up from New Brighton. It was the signal that the Liverpool lifeboat was required. The alarm was immediately spread to the adjoining Prince's landing stage. Mr. Corfield, Superintendent of the Liverpool lifeboats had, however, seen the distress rocket himself.

Mr. Corfield and the crew of the Liverpool lifeboat had, in accordance with the instructions of Lt. Sweny , Marine Surveyor to the MDHB, been on watch at the Prince's landing stage from 8.00 pm that evening. Upon sighting the first rocket around 11.05 pm. Mr. Corfield summoned the crew of the Liverpool lifeboat.

Hastily putting on their oilcoats, leggings and cumbersome cork life-jackets, it appeared to onlookers that the lifeboat men were in competition with one another to be first to man the boat, so urgent were their actions.

One of the crew, John 'Leggy` Gannon was unique to the lifeboat service, having only one leg, but he got about as ably as any man with the aid of a crutch and to quote his fellow lifeboatmen, John Gannon is a stout old sea dog who loves the dangers of the deep, and has, on more than one occasion done good service, going out to rescue human life. At the time, Leggy had served 15 years in the lifeboat service. With as little delay as possible the Liverpool No. 2 lifeboat, which was hanging from the davits, at the south end of the stage, was manned and launched, Leggy Gannon being one of the first aboard.

The stage master had, in the meantime, ordered a blue light to be burned; this being the signal used to gain the services of a tug boat to take the lifeboat out to sea. There were at that time over a dozen tugs at anchor in the river and as a rule there was no problem in obtaining the services of a steam tug to assist the lifeboats.

Nicholas Hinchley, Coxswain of the Liverpool No. 2 lifeboat - or Captain as the MDHB coxswains were more commonly called - and his crew of 12, as soon as their boat was afloat, cleared her away for sea and made ready for towing out.

The Liverpool lifeboat was a fine conventional Liverpool type boat, 34 foot in length, diagonally planked and carrying 12 oars.

27

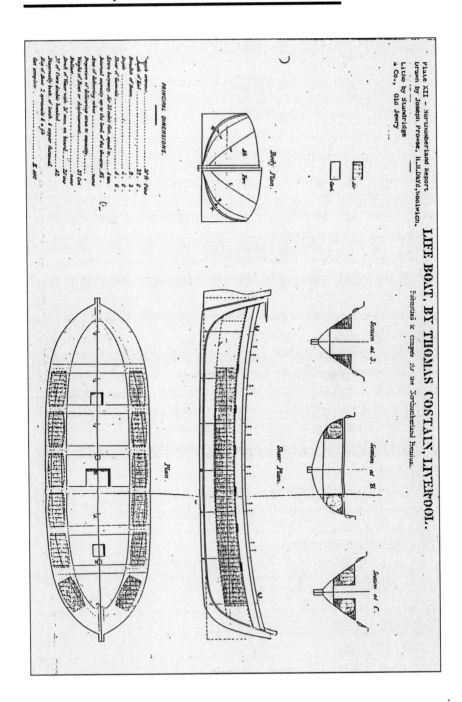

She was built in 1880 by Costain whose boats were primarily designed for towing. The Liverpool lifeboatmen preferred this boat to both the Tubular lifeboat which at that time was already afloat and secured at the back of the landing stage and to the Liverpool No. 1 lifeboat, which they claimed was too heavy in pulling. They had over the years been out many times in the Liverpool No. 2 boat and held a great fondness for her.

From the south end of the stage the lifeboat crew, taking to their oars, pulled to the small stage where the Customs launches berthed. Here lights were put aboard the lifeboat. They then proceeded to the north end of the stages where they assumed a tugboat would be waiting to tow them out. Owing to the violence of the storm and the quarter from which it blew, this short journey took a lot longer than usual, and great was their annoyance when it became apparent that no tug had been made available for them.

When the first distress rocket (fired from New Brighton) was sighted at Liverpool, Mr. Corfield, having first supervised the manning and launching of the lifeboat, had at once applied to the Master of the steam tug *Spindrift*, laying at the south end of the stage, to tow the Liverpool lifeboat. This, the *Spindrift*'s Master informed the lifeboat superintendent, he could not do, having already been engaged to stand by the Atlantic steamers *City of Paris* (of the Inman & International Steam Ship Co.) and *S.S. Alaska* (Owners Guion S.S. Co. Ltd.)[1]

As at New Brighton, a large crowd had gathered at the north end of the stage, attracted by the burning blue lights which could be seen all over the river, and by the red distress rockets continuously discharged by Mr. Brett at the New Brighton station, indicating that the Liverpool lifeboat was still urgently required, as were the services of a tug for the New Brighton boat. For despite the repeated firing of distress rockets no tug boats had been made available to either lifeboat station.

By 11.30 pm., some 25 minutes after Coxswain Martin had fired the first distress rocket, it became evident to the New

The south end of the Liverpool landing stage in the 1890s.

The Atlantic steamer 'City of Paris', Inman and International S.S. Co.
See footnote 1.

Brighton lifeboatmen and the crowds of onlookers, that by the continuous display of blue lights the Liverpool lifeboat was also unable to secure the services of a tug. The excitement among the crowd was now intense, with red distress rockets being repeatedly discharged at New Brighton, and blue lights burning and other signals being let off at Liverpool. It was now very obvious to all that the need for immediate assistance was great.

The lifeboatmen sitting in their respective boats were powerless to render any assistance until they were towed out. And being able to see so many tugs at anchor in the river with their lights burning and steam up, served to turn .heir patience into anger and frustration at this unnecessary waste of valuable time in getting to the aid of the unfortunate sailors aboard the stranded *Maxwell*.

Nicholas Hinchley, coxswain of the Liverpool boat, out of sheer frustration ordered his crew to row down to the *Spindrift* and there appealed to her crew to go and secure the services of a tug for them. With this, and the urgent request of the Pier Master, the *Spindrift* slipped her moorings at once and in a very short time had acquired the services of the steam paddle tug *Kingfisher*. Owned by John Shaw Turnbull of the Liverpool Steam Tug Company, she was a much more powerful tugboat and faster than the *Spindrift*, which made her very suitable for towing the lifeboat out in such adverse conditions in the quickest possible time.

As the crew of *Kingfisher* prepared to take the lifeboat in tow *Spindrift* made all speed back to the landing stage, where her Master informed Mr. Corfield that the *Kingfisher* was at his disposal. The message was quickly relayed to the crew of the lifeboat, with the Master of the *Spindrift* offering to tow them over to the *Kingfisher*. The offer was immediately accepted. Mr. Corfield then instructed Coxswain Martin of the Liverpool No.1 lifeboat (no relation to William Martin, Coxswain of the New Brighton boat) to have refreshments made ready for the No 2 crew on return from their mission. Mr. Corfield then boarded the

Spindrift and the Liverpool No. 2 boat, was taken out into the river to the *Kingfisher* were Mr. Corfield transferred to her for the tow out to sea.

It did not take long for the crews of *Kingfisher* and the lifeboat, once *Spindrift* had cleared away, to secure the 35 fathom tow line between them, then with the cheers of the onlookers ringing in their ears and many hearty good wishes to the success of their mission being raised, not withstanding the delay, they finally got under way around 11.40 pm.

At about the same time, the tug *Great Western*, inward bound from the stranded *Maxwell*, and passing close to New Brighton pier, was hailed, and coming about, took the -New Brighton lifeboat in tow and proceeded at once back towards the Bar and the wreck of the *Maxwell*, much to the relief of the lifeboat crew and the delight of the crowd. Now at last, after a delay of some 35 minutes from the first distress rocket being fired from New Brighton, help was on its way.

The delay in obtaining the services of a steam tug to tow the Liverpool lifeboat out would never have occurred a few years prior to the event. It was then the policy of the Dock Board to pay a retaining fee for one of the old tug company's boats. This ensured that a tug boat was always lying at the landing stage night and day, with steam up ready to proceed immediately the services of the lifeboat were required; the retaining fee was about £15 per day. Once hired the duty lifeboat tug would not undertake any other work for that day. The flag boat, as it was called, was then one of the most familiar sights at the landing stage, its dingy ensign being pointed out to visitors as evidence of the care with which the Mersey Docks & Harbour Board provided for the safety of seafarers using the Port of Liverpool. The services of the flag boat were discontinued for economic reasons.

At midnight on this terrible night the wind shifted once again, this time veering from the north east to north. Although the wind strength dropped slightly it was still blowing a heavy gale.

Into the teeth of the gale, and with an exceptionally high sea running, the steam paddle tugs *Great Western* and *Kingfisher* with the New Brighton and Liverpool lifeboats in tow, forged ahead with all possible speed, out towards the Crosby lightship, all receiving a severe buffeting.

The Liverpool lifeboat was shipping a lot of water, but this caused the crew no real problem, the water quickly leaving automatically through two non-return valves set in the boat's bottom.

The tug *Kingfisher* being the faster of the two tugs soon over- hauled the *Great Western*. On reaching the Crosby lightship, Coxswain Hinchley hailed the crew to ascertain the whereabouts of the wreck; back came the reply that a vessel was aground on Little Burbo Bank. With this information the tow was resumed, the Master of the *Kingfisher* easing his tug and tow around Crosby Bend.

Now with the wind and sea on their starboard side they set course towards the Mersey Bar, with *Great Western* and *Henry Richardson* following in their wake. Both lifeboats were rolling and swooping violently, with great sheets of spray bursting over their starboard gunwales to be whipped away with such force by the screaming wind that it sounded like hailstones beating against the oilskins and sou'westers of the lifeboatmen and felt like needle jabs when it lashed against exposed faces and hands, turning them numb. But now at least the Liverpool No. 2 boat was not shipping as much water as when she was ploughing head on into the sea.

The two tugs were not faring much better than their charges, with their great paddles beating thin air as they were lifted clear of the water each time the huge seas rolled them near on to their beam ends. It sent them over to port then back to starboard, burying their rails in the boiling sea with each roll and leaving the tug boat men hanging on as best they could. Be it at the helm, on the towing deck or in the engine rooms, they carried out their

33

various duties as best as they could to ensure that this gallant little convoy should continue on its mission of mercy. Later Coxswain Hinchley, who had then been 11 years in the lifeboat service, was to say it was the worst storm and most terrible seas that most of them had ever experienced in all their years as seamen and lifeboatmen.

Slowly but surely they forged ahead; Bidston Hill Observatory recorded wind speeds that July night of eighty to one hundred miles an hour. Out past the Formby lightship they struggled and on into Queens Channel. As the *Kingfisher* and the Liverpool lifeboat neared the Bar buoys the men aboard both vessels strained to penetrate the ink black night with eyes sore from the effects of salt and spray, and at last the wreck was sighted.

They could see she was a full rigged sailing ship, laying sunk just southward of the Bar, between No. 1 and No. 2 red conical buoys. She lay with a noticeable list to port with her mast and very little else above water, even the poop deck now being awash. With massive seas continually breaking over her, it seemed to those observing her that she would not last much longer under such an onslaught, and no time must be lost in securing the safety of her crew, all of whom had now taken refuge in the rigging including Captain Fraser who had climbed into the mizzen mast rigging when the poop deck had become awash.

As *Kingfisher* struggled to haul the Liverpool lifeboat to windward of the wreck, the crew of the *Maxwell* saw the lifeboat for the first time as she was lifted atop a huge wave, and for the first time since going aground nearly three hours earlier, they felt some hope for their safety.

It was now 2.00am. on the morning of July 20th 1892. It had taken the *Kingfisher* just under two and a half hours to cover a distance of some thirteen miles, in one of the worst storms ever recorded in the Mersey Estuary, to bring the Liverpool lifeboat out to the wreck. About 300 yards to windward of the *Maxwell*, Coxswain Hinchley signalled the tug to cast them off, then taking to their oars the Liverpool lifeboat dropped down, stern first, toward the sunken ship.

Battling through that massive, confused sea was a terrible strain but the men stuck with their task with grim determination. As they neared the ship the boat's anchor was made ready to let go. Then, rounding by the stern of the *Maxwell* and about to get alongside the wreck to leeward, they were hit by three tremendous seas. They rode over the first two but the third wave struck the Liverpool lifeboat on the starboard bow and side, throwing her completely over to port.

The oars and everything in the boat were carried away and all the men thrown into the raging sea. Then commenced a terrible struggle for life.

The boat remained afloat, bottom up. Those who could, clambered onto the capsized boat and clung to her keel, others in the water clung to her sides hanging onto grab lines or anything else they could so as not to be swept away into that pitch black hell of a night.

The New Brighton lifeboat arrived on the scene very shortly after the capsize of the Liverpool boat. Having worked her way to windward of the wreck, the *Great Western* let go of the New Brighton lifeboat. Demonstrating great skill and seamanship, Coxswain Martin and his crew, after much difficulty in running down to the ship, dropped anchor under her stern and succeeded in reaching the leeside of the *Maxwell.* One by one the *Henry Richardson's* brave crew took off her crew until only Captain Fraser remained aboard his ship.

When lifted atop a big wave, those men of the Liverpool lifeboat who had climbed onto her upturned hull could see the New Brighton men making their approach to the wreck. The two boats were within hailing distance, but the cries for assistance from the Liverpool men were drowned in the roar of the elements, and their frantic waving to attract attention went unseen in the darkness as slowly they drifted away into the night, driven by the howling wind and the turbulent seas.

Captain Fraser (for some reason known only to himself), having seen his crew safely transferred to the lifeboat steadfastly refused to leave his ship. No entreaties or threats from Coxswain Martin or the lifeboat's crew could move him.

At great risk to himself, one of the lifeboatmen climbed into the rigging where Captain Fraser had taken refuge, telling the Captain that they would not leave without him, and pointing out to him the danger the lifeboat and its occupants were in the longer they remained alongside the *Maxwell*, the lifeboat having nearly capsized twice already. At this, the Captain promised to leave the stricken ship.

The lifeboatman left the wreck first and having gained the safety of the lifeboat he beckoned Captain Fraser to follow him. As the *Henry Richardson* rose on the crest of a wave the Captain seized his chance and jumped into the boat, badly bruising himself in doing so. He lay half conscious until - as he later recalled - someone poured some rum into his mouth, which, he said, tasted more like Stockholm tar[2].

Now with all 29 members of the *Maxwell's* crew safely aboard the New Brighton lifeboat, Coxswain Martin had his crew haul her away from the wreck. Once clear they made small sail and steered their way back towards the *Great Western*, rendezvousing with her near the Crosby lightship. It was indeed a most gallant rescue by the crew of the *Henry Richardson*, carried out to perfection in hazardous and extreme conditions.

Notes:-

1. Due to the severity of the weather both the *City of Paris* and the *Alaska* were moved off the landing stage and moored off the north end of the stages.

2. During the course of the rescue, Captain Fraser's cash box containing £1,200 was thrown to the lifeboat, but by some mishap fell between the two vessels and was lost.

Overleaf (P38): A chart (not to scale), of Liverpool Bay circa 1875, showing the approximate positions of the some of vessels involved that fateful night in 1892.

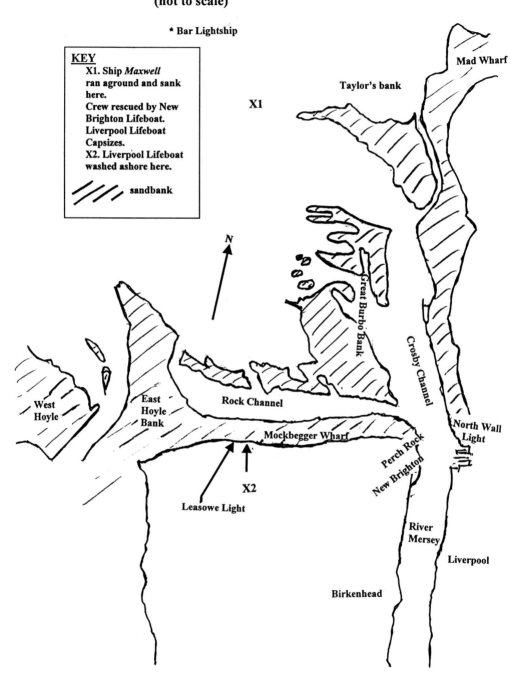

LIVERPOOL BAY circa 1875
(not to scale)

* Bar Lightship

KEY
X1. Ship *Maxwell* ran aground and sank here.
Crew rescued by New Brighton Lifeboat.
Liverpool Lifeboat Capsizes.
X2. Liverpool Lifeboat washed ashore here.

///// sandbank

Mad Wharf

Taylor's bank

X1

N

Great Burbo Bank

Crosby Channel

West Hoyle

East Hoyle Bank

Rock Channel

Mockbegger Wharf

North Wall Light

Leasowe Light

X2

Perch Rock

New Brighton

River Mersey

Liverpool

Birkenhead

Chapter Four

The loss of Liverpool No.2 boat

The tug *Kingfisher* remained cruising about the area where she had cast off the Liverpool lifeboat, her Captain fully expecting that she would shortly be hailed once the crew of *Maxwell* had been taken off. But as time wore on and the lifeboat did not reappear, Mr. Corfield became anxious for the safety of the boat. As the dawn approached and they could see well enough, they began to search for the missing lifeboat.

The crew of the *Kingfisher* recalled that when the Liverpool lifeboat was cast off the sea was wild and the night so dark that nothing could be seen or heard from the tug. Consequently no one aboard the *Kingfisher* saw the lifeboat capsize, and no cry for help was heard above the howling wind.

Shortly after *Kingfisher* began her search for the Liverpool boat her crew saw the New Brighton lifeboat leaving the *Maxwell* with the survivors. *Kingfisher* followed and asked if they had seen anything of the No. 2 lifeboat; Coxswain Martin informed them that they had seen nothing of her. *Kingfisher* then turned back and resumed the search looking in all directions, both likely and unlikely, for the missing lifeboat.

The *Henry Richardson* having re-joined the tug *Great Western* was once again taken in tow for the long haul back towards the mouth of the river. The exhausted but jubilant crews of both the lifeboat and the tug, and the rescued sailors from the *Maxwell* were all unaware of the fate that had befallen the Liverpool lifeboatmen.

When the crew of the capsized lifeboat realised that they had not been seen, and that their cries for help had gone unheard by the crew of the *Henry Richardson* they knew that the only chance of survival was to stay with their boat. Those of the crew that had managed to climb onto the upturned hull set about making their positions more secure, and to help as best they could those men still in the water. Some of the men had been injured when the boat capsized and could do little or nothing to help themselves, others were suffering from shock and exposure.

The night was so dark that the lifeboatmen could not see if any of their comrades were missing. In this condition they drifted before the wind, while the sea dashed over them incessantly. Bodies numbed with cold and pounded by the merciless sea, a few poor souls lost their grip and slipped back into the water, to be grasped just in time by one of their fellows and hauled back onto the hull.

At some time between the *Maxwell* grounding and midnight, the Isle of Man paddle steamer *Mona's Isle III*, inward bound from Douglas to Liverpool and carrying a large number of passengers, narrowly escaped collision with the wreck. Only the sharp lookout kept by her crew, and the great presence of mind and admirable seamanship displayed by Captain Ruthin, her Master, when the wreck was first sighted, saved by the closest of margins what would have been a terrible disaster.

The *Mona's Isle III* had sailed from Douglas at 4.30 p.m. on July 19th 1892. During her passage to Liverpool the weather grew progressively worse until she bore the full force of the storm, losing the use of one paddle. Her crew somehow managed to set some sail and with the combination of power and sail Captain Ruthin maintained his course at a greatly reduced speed, passengers and crew experiencing much discomfort.

When news first reached Liverpool that a large ship was in distress at the Bar, it was widely assumed that it was the *Mona's Isle III* , she being some 3 hours overdue when the first distress rockets were sighted at Formby and New Brighton.

Officials from the Isle of Man Steam Packet Company, along with relatives and friends of the passengers and crew were gathered at the landing stage to await her arrival and now became extremely anxious for news of her. Much to everyone's relief she was sighted coming up river at one o'clock in the morning of July 20th. She eventually made fast in her berth at the Liverpool landing stage four hours after her estimated time of arrival. It had been for all aboard her a voyage to remember.

During all of this time the Formby lifeboat had continued on its mission of mercy, pulling through mountainous seas towards the Mersey Bar, with her Coxswain John Aindow urging his crew on with every stroke of their oars until, after a nightmarish passage, the distressed ship was at last reached. The crew of the Formby lifeboat could see no signs of life aboard the wreck and surmised that either the New Brighton or Liverpool lifeboat had taken off her crew. The wind was still northerly and although it had lost a little of its strength it was still blowing very hard.

Having assured himself that there was nobody left aboard the *Maxwell,* Coxswain Aindow[1] thought it advisable to stay out in the channel so as to be able to give immediate assistance to any other vessel that might find herself in any difficulty. The decision made, the Formby lifeboat proceeded to patrol between the Formby and Crosby lightships for the rest of the night.

Mona's Isle III. On July 19th 1892 some time between the sailing ship Maxwell grounding and sinking on the night of the 19th and dawn of 20th, she was inward bound from Douglas to Liverpool and carrying many passengers, narrowly escaped running into the 'Maxwell". The sharp look out kept by the Mona's Isle III crew and the admirable seamanship of Captain Ruthin when the wreck was sighted, averted a terrible disaster, the vessels being so close they almost shaved.

She was the first of five similar steel paddle steamers built for the Isle of Man Steam Packet Co. and added to the fleet between 1882-1889. She was at the time, the largest, best appointed and most expensive steamer in the company's history. Exceptionally fast in her day, she could reach Liverpool from Douglas in 3 hours and 35 minutes. In 1915 she was sold to the Admiralty and saw much active service in World War I.

The Isle of Man Steam Packet Company did not buy her back.

During her search for the Liverpool lifeboat, the *Kingfisher* came upon the Formby lifeboat. Mr. Corfield spoke with John Aindow, asking for news of the Liverpool lifeboat only to receive the same answer as the New Brighton lifeboatmen had given, that they had seen nothing of the Liverpool No. 2 boat. *Kingfisher* resumed her search directed by Mr. Corfield, cruising right to the back of the Great Burbo bank near to the Horse Channel without any success.

The Formby lifeboat maintained her lone vigil between the two lightships for several more hours, but fortunately her services were not called on. Her crew, now totally exhausted returned to their station at 10.00a.m., more than ten hours after being launched. As dawn broke over the storm tossed waters of the Mersey Estuary on that morning of July 20th it was to bear witness to the pitiful plight of the Liverpool lifeboatmen, still left clinging with a death-fearing tenacity to their upturned boat.

With the coming of dawn a count was made of the men still with the boat. Of the thirteen who had embarked some four and a half hours earlier, two were missing. Of the eleven survivors, seven were injured, three of them seriously.

When the Liverpool lifeboat capsized, pitching her crew into the sea, Emmanuel Rodriguez, before he had any chance of gaining a hold on the upturned lifeboat, was swept away, never to be seen alive again.

After a tremendous struggle, made worse by their oilskins, heavy sea boots and cumbersome cork life-jackets, to say nothing of the injuries most of the men had sustained, the rest of the crew managed to reach the comparative safety of the capsized boat. William Ruffler, John 'Leggy` Gannon, David Thomas and Henry Beaver all managed to get onto the upturned hull. Leggy Gannon maintained a strong grip on the boat's keel with one hand and hung onto his crutch with the other. William Ruffler, exhausted by his ordeal, had no strength left and very soon after gaining his position on the hull he was washed off and vanished into the night.

43

David Thomas, as soon as he had climbed onto the hull inserted his hand into one of the non-return valve outlets and several of the men clung to his legs and oilskins. As the light grew stronger and the lifeboatmen could see about them more clearly it was soon realised that some of the men were in very poor shape, particularly Daniel Morgan, John Gavin and Albert Martin. Their colleagues did what they could to help and comfort their comrades but in the circumstances they could do very little to ease the suffering.

It became obvious to those helping to support Morgan that he was becoming delirious and soon he lost consciousness. John Gavin had a badly injured knee and although he remained conscious he soon became completely helpless. Albert Martin, although badly injured was more able to help himself as he too gained a position on the bottom of the boat with assistance and encouragement from his fellows. Charles Norton and John Hughes had also been injured, but like Martin, fought against the elements and their injuries to reach the boat. William Bramhall who had injured both hands also managed to regain the boat. Of the thirteen who had manned the Liverpool No. 2 boat only four had escaped any physical injury, they were her Coxswain, Nicholas Hinchley, William Ellison, David Thomas and Henry Beaver.

As the new day dawned, Coxswain Samuel Armitage with the Hoylake lifeboat was sighted by the Liverpool lifeboatmen, making her way out towards the wreck. Once again they had their hopes of rescue raised. Those who were most able shouted and waved frantically, but it was all to no avail as the Hoylake boat maintained her course out towards the *Maxwell* unaware that the *Maxwell's* crew had already been rescued. The Liverpool men had again gone unnoticed by their fellow lifeboatmen.

The tug *Kingfisher*, having spoken to both the New Brighton and the Formby lifeboats during her search for the missing lifeboat, had continued her search, but after several hours Mr.

Corfield and the master of *Kingfisher* decided it was futile to continue. The decision made, the tug was proceeding back towards Liverpool when she came upon the half wrecked and dismasted schooner *Rambler* of Preston, laying approximately one and a half miles westward of the northwest buoy. Although anchored she was dragging badly.

Rambler was the vessel that had run into the *Maxwell* with such force shortly after she had grounded some six hours earlier. Somehow she had stayed afloat throughout that terrible night, her crew totally helpless to do anything except to hang on and pray. The force of the collision and the continuous onslaught of the sea had carried away her mast, yards, booms, sails and rigging but miraculously all her crew were accounted for.

It was decided by the master of the *Kingfisher* to take *Rambler* in tow. It did not take long to secure a towline between the two vessels, although some difficulty was experienced in weighing *Rambler*'s anchors. Once this had been achieved *Kingfisher* with the battered *Rambler* in tow continued her passage back towards Liverpool.

At approximately 5 o'clock that same morning, the tug *Great Western* along with the New Brighton lifeboat *Henry Richardson* arrived off New Brighton pier. Most of the crew of the *Maxwell* were then transferred from the lifeboat to the tug for passage to Liverpool. Captain Fraser and one crewmember were landed at New Brighton where a kindly policeman took the Captain into his care and escorted him along New Brighton pier to the Promenade, from where a horse cab took the Captain to his nephew's house. The *Great Western* then made the short trip up river to the Liverpool landing stage where the *Maxwell*'s crew were put ashore. The shipwrecked sailors made a pitiful sight as they landed freezing cold and soaked to the skin, they had lost all their effects when their ship had sunk, leaving them with only the gear they now stood in.

Mr. Hanmer of the Liverpool Sailors' Home provided many of

them with new clothing, while others received help from the Shipwrecked Mariners Aid Society. The men of the *Henry Richardson* [2], once their boat was secure and made ready for the next call out, and their reports made, were at last able to take a well-earned rest. The steam tug *Great Western* [3], her services no longer required, returned to her berth, her crew having been on continuous duty for more than 24 hours. Only those who have experienced such weather conditions at sea in small ships and have worked through them for many hours without respite can begin to imagine what the crews of these vessels had endured, and how they felt at the end of it all.

When Lt. Sweny R.N., Senior Marine Surveyor for the MDHB was informed of the rescue of the *Maxwell* 's crew and that the *Kingfisher* was searching for the missing Liverpool lifeboat, he immediately acquired the services of the steam tug *Brilliant Star* to take him out to the wreck with all speed. After a quick but rough passage *Brilliant Star* arrived in the vicinity of the wreck but there was no sign of human life.

After a brief search Lt. Sweny came to the conclusion that the lifeboat, unable to regain the tug *Kingfisher* after attempting to take off the *Maxwell* 's crew, had proceeded back to Liverpool under sail or by pulling by way of the Rock Channel that lay some 8 miles to the south east of the wreck. This was much used by shallow drafted vessels plying trade between the North Wales coast and Liverpool. With this consideration, Lt. Sweny requested the master of the *Brilliant Star* to return to Liverpool.

Crew members from the sailing ship *Maxwell* taken off by the New Brighton lifeboat *Henry Richardson* 20th July 1892.

T.G. Fraser of Caithness Drive, Liscard. (Captain)

R.G. Mowatt of 89 Arundel Street, Liverpool. (Mate)

A.G. Mason of Kingston upon Thames, Surrey. (Second Mate)

J.C. McGreery of Cumberland. (Boatswain)

W.H. Dailey of County Road, Liverpool. (Boatswain's Mate)

J. Macrae of Banffshire, Scotland. (Carpenter)

J.Humphrey of Whitehaven. (Sailmaker)

A.de Silva of Cornwallis St., Liverpool. (Steward)

D.Smith of Cornwallis St., Liverpool (Cook)

A.Kitchen of Whitehaven. (A.B.)

F.F. Carsten of 23 Duke St., Liverpool. (A.B.)

P. Vonthin of 23 Duke St., Liverpool. (A.B.)

C.E. Boldt of 61 Paradise St., Liverpool. (A.B.)

0. Dering of 61 Paradise St., Liverpool. (A.B.)

W. Hoffstrorn of 23 Duke St., Liverpool. (A.B.)

R. Cardwell of 23 Duke St., Liverpool. (A.B.)

W. Bonner of Steble Grove, Liverpool. (A.B.)

A. Birtrin of 62 Pitt St., Liverpool. (A.B.)

A. Yansen of 62 Pitt St., Liverpool. (A.B.)

J. Nilesen of 62 Pitt St., Liverpool. (A.B.)

J.F. Kirkham of Madryn St., Liverpool. (A.B.)

R. Graydon of Dickenson St., Liverpool. (A.B.)

0. Armstrong of 19 Kent St., Liverpool. (A.B.)

J. Wilson of 8 Toxteth St., Liverpool. (A.B.)

I.A. Glover of Greenhithe, Kent. (A.B.)

R.B. Rankin of Cardiff. (Apprentice)

G.H. Pierson of London. (Apprentice)

J.H. Tripp of London. (Apprentice)

J. Radwood of Liverpool. (Apprentice)

The steam paddle tug "Great Western".

At 5.30 a.m. on July 19th 1892 the tug Great Western took the full rigged sailing ship Maxwell in tow at Birkenhead Docks for the long haul out to the north west lightship. At 11.00 p.m. that night the Maxwell struck the Little Burbo Bank and sank in hurricane conditions while trying to re-cross the Bar, still under tow of the Great Western. The tug proceeded back to Liverpool for assistance. In the early hours of July 20th she returned to the wreck with the New Brighton lifeboat Henry Richardson in tow. The New Brighton boat succeeded in rescuing all 29 of Maxwell's crew. At approximately 5.00 a.m. the Great Western arrived back off New Brighton with the New Brighton lifeboat in tow. The Maxwell's crew with the exception of Captain Fraser and one other member, were transferred from the lifeboat to the Great Western for passage to Liverpool, Captain Fraser and his colleague being landed at New Brighton.

The Great Western official number 76362 was built in 1876 at Renfrew, Scotland for W. & M. Jolliffe of Liverpool. Built of iron, she measured 154.2ft. x 23.7ft. x 12.7 ft. and weighed 300 tons.

Sold by Jolliffe in 1898, she was wrecked in collision in the River Mersey December 27th 1898, Captain R. Griiffiths.

48

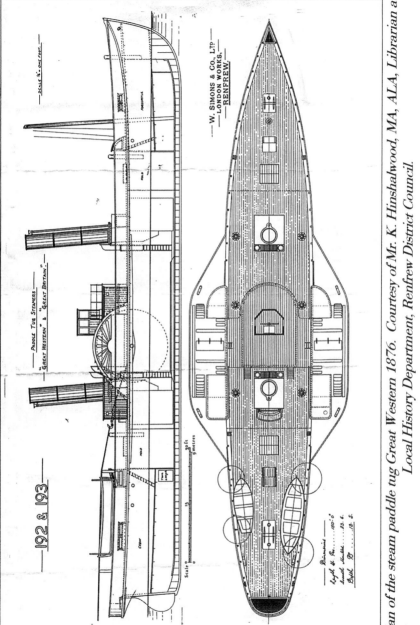

Plan of the steam paddle tug Great Western 1876. Courtesy of Mr. K. Hinshalwood, MA, ALA, Librarian at Local History Department, Renfrew District Council.

The New Brighton Lifeboat Henry Richardson, under oar and fully manned on exercises off New Brighton C1890s.
(Courtesy RNLI)

The New Brighton lifeboat Henry Richardson seen here at the Lowestoft sailing lifeboat trials 1892. Built at Barrow in 1888 at a cost of £625 she was the largest of the tubular lifeboats - 43ft. long and 12ft. in the beam, and carried a crew of 16.

On the night of July 19th 1892 the Henry Richardson coxswain, William Martin, was towed out to the wreck of the Maxwell by the steam paddle tug Great Western. Reaching the wreck after the Liverpool No. 2 lifeboat, she succeeded in rescuing all 29 crew from the stranded vessel.

The steam paddle tug Brilliant Star.

On the morning of July 19th 1892 the Brilliant Star took the New Brighton lifeboat 'Henry Richardson' in tow and proceeded to Formby Channel to the assistance of the three masted schooner Renown (owners, A.C. Shaw, Runcorn), aground at Formby Hole.
Just over 24 hours later on the morning of July 20, after the New Brighton lifeboat had returned with the survivors from the wrecked Maxwell, the Brilliant Star took Lt. Sweny, senior Marine Surveyor for the MDHB out to the wreck site in search of the Liverpool No. 2 lifeboat, without success.
Brilliant Star was built in 1876 at South Shields by J.P. Rennoldson & Sons Ltd. for Mr. Harry Strong of Liverpool.
Sold to Mr. William Becket Hill in 1900 when Mr. Strong went out of business, she was in service until 1905.
Hill's tugs later became the famous Cock tugs, Liverpool screw, towing and lighterage.

Photograph courtesy Mr. P.N. Thomas, tug historian.

Meanwhile the Liverpool lifeboat had continued to drift stern first in a wide westerly sweep towards the Rock Channel. As time slowly passed the men had grown weaker in body but not in spirit, nor in the will to live. In the two hours since the capsize their position had been one of constant danger and hardship, mixed with bitter frustration, their hopes being raised one moment by the sighting of other lifeboats, only to be dashed with the terrible realisation that they had gone unheard and unseen, and all in the knowledge that the further they drifted away from the main channels the less the chance they would be sighted by other vessels.

The wind still blew from the north and the huge seas continued, but slowly and mercifully the wind strength was moderating and the sea becoming less wild, although the waves still washed over the boat at regular intervals. The rigours of the lifeboatmen's ordeal were now becoming painfully obvious, with limbs starting to swell through injury and the constant pounding of the water that drove their bodies against the hull. Hands and wrists were swollen through the sheer effort of hanging on for dear life. William Bramhall endured mind-numbing pain throughout the night in his bid for survival, with both hands already badly injured. Daniel Morgan was now very close to death, but his fellows, using one hand to save themselves, clung to him with the other, grimly determined that the sea would not claim him.

The same battle for life was taking place with those men nearest to John Gavin, as his semiconscious body grew heavier as they grew weaker. Leggy Gannon somehow managed not only to maintain his grip on the boat's keel, but also kept a firm grip on his crutch. Although a powerfully built man, he felt his strength slowly ebbing away as the night wore on. David Thomas who had inserted his hand into the non-return valve was now finding the strain on his hand and wrist too much to maintain the combined weight of his own body and that of his comrades, who still clung to his legs and oilskins in their struggle for survival. But Thomas,

53

sooner than shake them off and make it safer for himself, instead forced his arm so deeply into the aperture that it became near impossible for him to let go. For hour after agonising hour throughout that fearful night, the safety of David Thomas and the men who clung to him depended upon his hold and all the time Thomas knew that at any moment his arm could be torn from his body, but in spite of the pain he was enduring, Thomas kept his hold.

For three more hours after sighting the Hoylake lifeboat at daybreak their position remained one of continuous peril and suffering. Driven before wind and sea they drifted to the south, across the great sandbanks that litter the Mersey Estuary, massive seas tumbling and roaring over them. Although the wind force had moderated slightly and the sea state become less confused, it was not enough to allow them any respite. Pounded by the waves and lashed by both spray and spindrift, they drifted on towards the Rock Channel, blinded with salt and choking with nausea as it blocked their throats and nostrils, numbed by pain and the effects of being continually drenched by the freezing cold sea. Thus the Liverpool No. 2 lifeboat with the remains of her courageous crew still clinging to her, and to one another, was swept into the Rock Channel. At about 7 o'clock, some five hours after capsizing, she was cast ashore still bottom up, onto Leasowe Beach near to Leasowe lighthouse. They had drifted some seven and a half miles.

There now commenced the final battle of survival for the Liverpool lifeboatmen. As their boat grounded, they either slid or were swept off the upturned hull into the surf that boiled onto the Leasowe foreshore. But this time their struggle was to get away from the boat that had been their only refuge before she crushed them as the waves lifted and tossed her like a piece of driftwood higher and higher up the beach, until she eventually came to rest upon the Leasowe embankment.

But now, mercifully, the men were not left to fight for their lives alone. Local fishermen and others attracted to the shore by the fury of the storm had seen the lifeboat being swept towards the beach. As the alarm was spread along the foreshore people sped down the beach towards the upturned hull. On reaching the water's edge, some plunged into the surf to assist the floundering lifeboatmen. With the aid of ropes and any other means available to them these intrepid people brought all the men ashore.

Daniel Morgan, John Gavin and Leggy Gannon were all completely helpless and had to be carried from the sea and up the beach, to be lain gently on the sand and comforted by their rescuers until transport arrived. The three men were first taken to the residence of Dr. Pierce of Hoylake who examined them and had them transferred to the cottage hospital in Carlton Terrace, Hoylake.

Albert Martin, Charles Norton and John Hughes were taken from the beach in a cart to a nearby farmhouse where their injuries and other needs were attended.

Coxswain Hinchley along with David Thomas (who had managed to extract his arm intact from the valve in the hull), William Ellison, Harry Beaver and William Bramhall found their way to the nearby summer camp for destitute boys [7]. Here the Superintendent and his staff treated the men with the utmost kindness and the keepers of Leasowe lighthouse provided attention and refreshments. After being revived with hot coffee and other refreshment, and provided with dry clothing they and the three who had received hospitality at the farmhouse were all taken to the local railway station and put on a train for Liverpool. On arrival at James Street station the two worst cases - Charles Norton and John Hughes - were immediately taken to the Northern Hospital where both were detained.

The six remaining, not requiring any further medical attention, made their way from the station on foot, being met by Coxswain Martin, Captain of the Liverpool No. 1 lifeboat, near the Marine Surveyor's office at Canning Place. Martin informed his colleagues that refreshments had been made ready for them at Simpson's Rooms and escorted them there. Although delighted to be greeting his colleagues once again he was sobered by the harrowing details of their ordeal especially on learning that some lives had been lost.

For his part, once the *Kingfisher* had taken the Liverpool lifeboat in tow, Martin had, in compliance with Mr. Corfield's instructions to have refreshments made ready for the men's return, gone to Mrs. Simpson's tea rooms on Mann Island to make the necessary arrangements. Mrs. Simpson was not available, but one of the ladies there agreed to keep the rooms open all night in order to be ready to supply the lifeboatmen with refreshment when they returned. Coxswain Martin had then returned to the landing stage, to wait in vain for the return of the No. 2 lifeboat.

Now, after a long and anxious night, reunited with his fellow lifeboatmen and given an account of the night's events by his opposite number Nicholas Hinchley, it was time for the survivors to be reunited with their loved ones and take a much needed rest. Reports, interviews and enquiries would all come later; for them at least, the worst part of their shared ordeal was over.

On arrival at the cottage hospital Daniel Morgan, John Gavin and Leggy Gannon (still with his crutch in tow), were received by Mr. F.M. Morine, who was in charge of the hospital, and Miss Emma Jackson, the Matron.

Miss Jackson and her staff did all they possibly could for the men, but Daniel Morgan was by now beyond help. After clinging to life for more than seven hours throughout the night, helped and encouraged all along the way by his fellow lifeboatmen, his rescuers at Leasowe and now finally by the medical staff at the cottage hospital, Daniel Morgan, now quite delirious, died just half an hour after gaining the warmth and safety of the hospital, never having regained consciousness. The only visible injury about his body was a slight wound on his face.

John Gavin was detained with a badly injured knee, he was to remain in hospital until July 26th. When carried ashore at Leasowe, Leggy Gannon was totally exhausted, but after only a few hours in the hospital he became quite vigorous, his main concern being to get back home as soon as possible. He was detained until later in the day, when a doctor declared him fit enough to leave.

Notes:-

1. The Formby lifeboat station was at the time still under the control of the MDHB Coxswain Aindow remained at Formby after the RNLI. took control of the station in 1894, serving as coxswain from 1891 - 1910.

2. The lifeboat *Henry Richardson* was in continuous service at New Brighton No. 2 station from 1888 - 1898.

3. The *Great Western* was sold by W..& J. Jolliff in 1898 and was wrecked after a collision in the River Mersey on 27 December that same year.

4. A few days after the disaster, five of the Liverpool lifeboatmen: Dave Thomas, Will Bramhall, Charles Norton, Harry Beaver and William Ellison, collected the sum of five shillings (25p.) between themselves and forwarded a Postal Order for that amount to Mr. Adam Rankine, the Hon. Treasurer of the summer camp at 3 Tithebarn Street, Liverpool with the message that it was to be used for the benefit of the camp, in appreciation of the kindness shown to them.

Various views of the Hoylake Lifeboat 1890.
See page 60 for details.

Notes on the Hoylake Lifeboat 1890.

Built in 1890 by Thomas Costain for the Mersey Docks & Harbour Board's Hoylake lifeboat station, this fine Liverpool class boat measuring 34ft. X 9ft. 9 ins. and carrying 12 oars was in all probability identical to the Liverpool No. 2 boat, she also being built by Costain in 1880 for the MDHB's Liverpool lifeboat station situated at the Prince's landing stage on the Liverpool side of the River Mersey. Costain's boats were built primarily for towing and had formed the backbone of the MDHB fleet since the 1840s, having been improved on from time to time.

The type was later adopted by the Royal National Lifeboat Institution as an alternative to their self righting boats, and became known as the *Liverpool.*

It was the Liverpool No. 2 lifeboat that went to the assistance of the sailing ship *Maxwell* with such tragic consequence on July 19 1892. The Liverpool type lifeboats remained in service with the MDHB until July 1 1894 when the Dock Board handed over its stations to the RNLI. It was agreed by both parties that of the five stations then maintained by the Board, the one at Liverpool landing stage be abolished.

The lifeboats owned by the MDHB were given numbers, but not names. Upon the Dock Board handing over its stations to the RNLI the Hoylake boat was given the name *Coard William Squarey,* her coxswain from 1890-1894 being Samuel Armitage. The Hoylake boat passed the capsized Liverpool boat, but her crew did not see her in spite of the efforts of the Liverpool men.

Photographs supplied by Mr. J.P. Morris, Hon. Archivist for the Lifeboat Enthusiasts' Society; historic notes courtesy Dr. Alan Scarth, Maritime History Dept., William Brown Libraries Liverpool and from The Tubular Lifeboats 1850-1939 ' by G.E. Farr.

Chapter Five

The Inquest

N ews of the disaster that had befallen the Liverpool No. 2 lifeboat spread quickly, and when it was reported that two of the lifeboat's crew were missing a watch was ordered to be kept along the coast for the bodies. The news of the disaster was greeted on both sides of the river with a great sense of sadness and grief at the loss of life and the suffering endured by men who had voluntarily risked their lives in a bid to save others. Greatest was the grief felt by the families of the dead men, and that shared by fellow lifeboatmen and sea-going authorities who felt that the disaster and consequent anguish and misery might have been averted had a tug boat been on standby ready to tow the lifeboat out as soon as her services were called upon.

Three widows and fifteen children now faced a future of

destitution and starvation with the loss of their bread winners, their only hope of salvation laying in the hands of charitable people and organisations.

Shortly before 1 o'clock that afternoon Lt. Sweny, RN and other Dock Board officials gathered at the Liverpool landing stage prior to boarding the MDHB steam paddle tender *Vigilant*. All highly praised the gallantry of the Liverpool lifeboat's crew and expressed great surprise that the men had been able to survive such a night. All were loud in their congratulations to David Thomas, for it was certain that several more casualties would have occurred had it not been for his unselfish presence of mind and great endurance. They were also quick to compliment the brave Leggy who had managed to save himself and his crutch.

Vigilant then left the landing stage and proceeded at full speed towards the *Maxwell*, the objective being to establish the exact position of the wreck and to ensure that she presented no hazard to vessels entering or leaving the port. Shortly after getting under way the *Vigilant* met with the paddle tug *Kingfisher* coming up river with the dismasted schooner *Rambler* in tow.

The steam paddle tender 'Vigilant.' This illustration shows her in her original state and was taken when she was in attendance on the Royal Yacht 'Victoria and Albert' whose taffrail is just visible.

The Vigilant (centre background) seen here in the Albert Dock circa 1900.

Vigilant was built for the MDHB in 1876 by Bowdler, Chaffer & Co. at Seacombe. In 1903 she was replaced by a new vessel to which her name was transferred, the old paddle tender being renamed Octopus. At the end of her service with the MDHB. she was sold to Richard Able & Co. Ltd. and converted to a sand barge, being renamed "W.S. Patterson". In May 1966 she was towed from Liverpool to Preston and broken up.

63

Mr. Corfield, Superintendent of the Liverpool lifeboats, and the Captain and crew of *Kingfisher* were incredulous when informed that the Liverpool No. 2 boat had capsized and that lives had been lost. The tugboatmen's fatigue was quickly replaced by anger and the bitter knowledge that they had been within hailing distance of the lifeboat when disaster had struck, but had seen and heard nothing. *Vigilant* resumed her passage out to the wreck whilst *Kingfisher*, her crew saddened by the events of the night, proceeded up river with the battered wreck that was *Rambler* to secure a safe berth for them both.

By now the weather had moderated considerably and the Mersey Estuary bore no resemblance to the maelstrom that had raged there not so many hours before. On reaching the wreck, Lt. Sweny and his colleagues set about fixing its precise position, and upon completion of their survey returned to the Liverpool landing stage, where Lieutenant Sweny went immediately to the Dock Board's office[1] at Canning place to make his report. Lt. Sweny's memo to the board stated that 'With the position in which this vessel (*Maxwell*) lies, it will neither be necessary nor desirable to have a watch vessel or wreck buoy stationed to guard the wreck`, although he considered the wreck to be an obstruction which impeded safe navigation in and around that part of the Channel. On receiving this intelligence, the Board issued a notice to mariners, warning of the wreck and giving her precise position.

The Board also wasted no time in approaching the Liverpool Salvage Association to make arrangements to take steps on behalf of the MDHB for salving the cargo and materials of the ship *Maxwell*, which included anchors, chains, sails, rigging gear and appliances of the vessel. Mr. Rundell the Salvage Association's representative inspected the wreck and reported his findings to the Association who in turn sent a copy to the MDHB through Lieutenant Sweny.

The report stated that in the opinion of Mr. Rundell, the *Maxwell*'s cargo consisting as it did of coal only, it would not pay the expense of recovery from the ship in her present position, but if she could be floated off, the cargo would have a certain value. In the meantime salvage men from the Association were put aboard the wreck to strike down her gear and a diver examined her forepart but found no damage.

The salvage men worked all that Wednesday night 20 July, unbending all sails on mizzen and main mast and striking down the main royal yard and mizzen top gallant and royal yard which were then loaded aboard one of the Salvage Association's tenders and ferried to Liverpool to be stored at the Canning pierhead.

During the course of the day a thorough inspection of the Liverpool No. 2 lifeboat, now high and dry on the Leasowe embankment, was carried out. Although all her gear had been lost, including the tiller, there was no structural damage to her hull.

Righted, the lifeboat was hauled down to the water's edge and refloated, then taken in tow by the MDHB tender *Alert*. She arrived back in Liverpool that evening and made fast in Canning Dock.

Late in the evening of that fateful day the body of William Ruffler, who had been snatched from the upturned hull by the stormy sea, was found on the Hoyle Bank and taken to the Leasowe mortuary. Emmanuel Rodriguez was now the only member of the lifeboat's crew still unaccounted for, a watch for his body being maintained.

The morning following the disaster the MDHB received a letter from Messrs. Johnston Sproule & Company (owners of the *Maxwell*) stating that they had given notice of Abandonment to the underwriters on the *Maxwell* and her freight. The Thames and Mersey Marine Insurance Co. Ltd. having undertaken to underwrite the ship then placed the immediate future of the *Maxwell* into the hands of the MDHB having agreed that the MDHB would be covered for all their charges and expenses in connection with the vessel and her cargo, that the vessel and cargo should be properly dealt with and that the Board should be indemnified against all claims.

The MDHB having made an agreement now instructed the Liverpool Salvage Association to explore the possibility of refloating the *Maxwell*.

Soon after this agreement had been made, the Board's tender *Alert* with the Water Bailiff Lt. Simpson RN,. and other Dock Board officials aboard, left the Prince's landing stage with the purpose of securing the position of the wreck against any further casualties from the passing of inward and outward-bound vessels during salvage operations. At the same time the Salvage Association's vessel *Mallard* and the vessel *Gleaner* belonging to Messrs. J. Gillbouy & Co., divers, sailed for the wreck. At the wreck site the *Maxwell* was taken in hand by the salvage men of the *Mallard* and the divers of the *Gleaner* all under the supervision of Captain Young of the Liverpool Salvage Association, who wasted no time in ordering divers down to inspect the hull for any underwater damage.

On completion of their inspection the divers reported that the vessel had, by reason of her going aground, bent her heel and rudder besides receiving a nasty rent in her bottom. She also had a hole 6 feet long by 2 feet wide on the port side of the poop deck where the schooner *Rambler* had collided with her at the height of the storm, but fortunately this was above the watermark. She had taken on a list of 11 degrees to port, so at low water her lee rail was just dry. With her sails and most of her upper yards being sent down she became much lighter overhead, which removed the danger of her capsizing in any sudden squall. The divers also confirmed that she had grounded on firm sand and consequently had not settled too deeply, as would have been the case if she had grounded on quick sands, also there had been no shift in her cargo.

With all these facts now placed before him, Captain Young sent a report to Lieutenant Sweny RN of the MDHB outlining the condition of the wreck and the salvage operations that would have to be carried out in order to refloat her. On the evidence of the report, the MDHB instructed the Liverpool Salvage Association to proceed.

Very few ships have ever been recovered from the treacherous tide swept sandbanks of the Mersey Estuary, but work towards that end began at once, the first task being to plug the gash in *Maxwell*'s bottom. Divers filled the aperture with oakum, which reduced the quantity of water entering her by half. Meanwhile a large party of men were employed to discharge the cargo out of the fore hold so that suction pumps could be positioned to discharge the water from within her. The *Maxwell*'s own pumps were not powerful enough to pump such a volume of water and were replaced by the salvage company's more powerful steam suction pumps. Before any pumping out could commence, the discharging of cargo from the fore hold had to be completed and the rents in the hull plugged. This work would take the salvage men the best part of two days.

On the day following the disaster the Lord Mayor of Liverpool, James de Bels Adam[2], issued an appeal on behalf of the widows and orphans of the lifeboatmen, intimating that he would be glad to receive donations, however small, for the purpose of assisting the wives and families of the men who had lost their lives and he hoped that any collections being made by associations or individuals would be forwarded to him in order that the money could be placed in a common fund. The Mayor also had a collecting box placed inside the railings at the entrance to the Town Hall for the receipt of small contributions from those who did not wish their names to appear in print. The weekly meeting of the MDHB held that same day at Canning Place was presided over by Mr. G.B. Crowe, other members present being Messrs. Barrow, Gladstone, Allen, Woodward, Hubback, Rathbone, Robertson, Watson, Bushell, Hughes, Kennedy, Crosfield, Henderson, Glynn, Chadwick, Fernie and Sir James Poole.

Referring to the accident, Mr. Crowe said that Mr. A.T. Squarey, the Board's solicitor, had taken some evidence from the Superintendent and one of the lifeboatmen, and requested him to read it.

Mr. Squarey addressing the meeting said that on Wednesday July 20th Mr. Corfield, Superintendent of lifeboats had made the statement, which he then read to the meeting. This covered the events leading up to and surrounding the capsize of the Liverpool No. 2 lifeboat, concluding that No. 2 was thought to be the handiest boat. No. 1 was not well liked by the men because she was too heavy in pulling. There was no prejudice against her capsizing. Mr. Corfield's statement went on to say that No. 2 had often been out in heavy weather and had never capsized before, all the lifeboat men liked her, and her crew were all experienced men. The report concluded: 'I do not think any blame attaches to anyone. I think it was just one ugly sea that hit the boat and turned her over.'

Mr. Squarey then read out the statement made by William Ellison, one of the men in the boat when she capsized: -

We went out with a full crew; twelve men and the master, to the wreck of the Maxwell. I had been out in the boat on many previous occasions in bad weather, and there was no reason at all to distrust her. When we let go we dropped down stern first to the wreck. The sea was very bad. We capsized just as we were about to let go our anchor in order to go alongside the wreck. A very big sea caught her on the starboard bow and side and rolled her over to port. I can't say that anyone was to blame, it was just an unusually big unlucky sea, and there was nothing at all amiss in the handling of the boat.

The statements having been read, the Chairman said that in view of the inquest to be held at Hoylake, the solicitor thought it undesirable that any discussion should take place on the subject until the verdict of the Coroner's jury was given. The meeting then moved on to other business.

The No. 2 lifeboat was moved from Canning dock the next day, once again by the tender *Alert*, to the Herculaneum dock, where she was completely overhauled before returning to service. During No. 2's absence from her station at the Prince's landing stage, her place was taken by a lifeboat formerly stationed at Hoylake, which was secured at the back of the landing stage and kept in readiness for any emergency.

While these events were in progress, the steam flat *John* of Liverpool[3] left the port for Greenfield, Flintshire. Once abeam of the Rock lighthouse she had come to port and proceeded out towards the Welsh coast by way of the Rock Channel. Late that same night as she slowly churned her way through the now peaceful waters of the Mersey Estuary, Captain Jones and his crew were very mindful of the tragic events that had taken place not 48 hours earlier, and a good look out was being maintained for anything out of the ordinary.

Their diligence was rewarded when wreckage was sighted and floating amidst the flotsam they found the body of Emmanuel Rodriguez. Once the body had been recovered from the sea, Captain Jones turned the *John's* head towards Holywell. The run to the land did not take long and the little steam flat was soon fast alongside at Llanerchymor, Holywell, where Captain Jones carried the body of Emmanuel Rodriguez ashore himself. It was then conveyed to the Packet House, Holywell to await formal identification.

The steam flat `Madge`. On Friday July 22 1892 the body of my great grandfather Emmanuel Rodriguez was picked up by a steam flat off the Welsh coast, two days after being cast adrift when the Liverpool lifeboat capsized.

Photograph courtesy of the Boat Museum, Ellesmere Port.

The Weaver steam packet steam flat `Bengal`. The steam flat was a steam powered version of the sailing Weaver flat - in other words a small and simple steam coaster. Easily converted from sail to steam by firms such as Yarwoods.

Photograph courtesy of the Boat Museum, Ellesmere Port.

71

Two Views of The Packet House, Greenfield, Holywell, Flintshire.

Having been carried ashore by Captain Jones of the steam flat 'John' the body of Emmanuel Rodriguez was taken by the authorities and laid here.

Julia Ann Rodriguez identified the body as that of her husband.

On Friday July 22nd Mr. Henry Churton, the West Cheshire Coroner, held an inquest at the Stanley Hotel, Hoylake, touching on the deaths of the two Liverpool lifeboatmen Ruffler and Morgan. Mr. Squarey, Mr. Miles K. Burton, Secretary, and Lt. Sweny the Marine Surveyor were present on behalf of the MDHB.

The first witness to be called was Miss Emma Jackson, matron of the cottage hospital Hoylake. In a brief statement to the Coroner, Miss Jackson said that the deceased man Morgan was admitted to the hospital at 9.15 on Wednesday morning July 20th; he was quite delirious, there were no marks or injuries on his body except for a slight wound on his face. Shortly after admission he went quiet and died half an hour later without regaining consciousness.

Mr. Squarey then informed the Coroner that the MDHB expressed deep regret that the lives of three very gallant men should have been sacrificed in the efforts they were making to save others. He also wished to inform the Coroner that the Dock Board would give every assistance it could in investigating the cause of the disaster. Also present at the inquest were the Superintendent of the Liverpool lifeboats, Coxswain Nicholas Hinchley of the No. 2 boat and Coxswain Martin of the No. 1 boat.

Mr. Martin had been requested to attend because of his experience in the lifeboat service; he knew the No. 2 boat well and would be prepared to answer any enquiries that might be put to him on the subject.

Nicholas Hinchley was the first witness from the lifeboat service to be called.

He explained the events of that terrible night, and said that he considered she was a splendid little boat to have carried them so far bottom up. He also informed the inquest that he considered the assistance given to them by the men on Leasowe shore in helping then out of the water ought to be recognised.

The Coroner then asked Coxswain Hinchley' Did the tug boat

stand by you after she cast you off?`

Hinchley replied that the *Kingfisher* stood out in the channel, expecting the lifeboat to come back from the ship, never expecting it to capsize. The lifeboat had to go along a bank where the tug could not follow, and at the time of the accident the tug was not within hail. He did not think there was any necessity for the tug to be nearer to render assistance, as had she been near she would probably have done more harm than good. Hinchley then went on to say that he had eleven years experience of the lifeboat and had never been out in a heavier sea than he experienced that night. A boat had never capsized before in his experience and he did not attach any blame to anyone for the unfortunate occurrence.

Mr. Churton then asked the jury if they considered it necessary to hear further evidence, pointing out that the Coxswain of the lifeboat had given a very clear and concise statement of what had taken place.

No further questions were asked. Coxswain Hinchley was then assisted from the room in a fainting condition, not having fully recovered from the effects of his ordeal. One of the jurymen then remarked upon the need for some provision to be made in case of such accidents, by which immediate medical attention could be obtained. The Coroner in reply said that if the jury had anything to recommend they could add it to their verdict by way of a rider, but so far as the cause of death was concerned the matter was very plain. There could be no doubt the two lifeboatmen lost their lives through an accident, and that the jury were not in a position to hold anybody responsible or to blame in the matter.

The foreman of the jury said they were quite satisfied with the evidence, but they wished to ask the gentlemen present connected with the Dock Board how it was they had not self righting lifeboats in their service? Replying for the MDHB Mr. Squarey said the men in this boat were exceedingly thankful it did not right itself on this occasion, as had it done so, they would all have gone to the bottom.

In reply to a question as to why the tubular boat was not taken out on the night in question Mr. Squarey explained than the men preferred the No. 2 lifeboat that was lighter. He further said that as to the question of a receiving house at Hoylake, that had never been presented to the Dock Board but at the same time it was out of the question to think of having medical aid established at every place at which a vessel might go ashore.

The Coroner, addressing the jury said that if they wished to make any presentment they could do so, and in the meantime he would leave them to their deliberations. After a brief discussion the jury returned a verdict of accidental death and added a rider suggesting that a receiving house be provided at Hoylake or such arrangements be made that in cases where men were exhausted by exposure immediate medical assistance might be obtained, either by placing the Leasowe lighthouse in telegraphic communication with Hoylake, or a room being provided at Leasowe or elsewhere, where such cases could be treated. With this, the inquest on William Ruffler and Daniel Morgan was closed. John Gavin who had been taken to the cottage hospital was reported to be doing well, now being a fair way towards recovery and his condition no longer critical. Charles Norton and John Hughes were also making good progress in the Northern hospital.

On the same day as the inquest in Hoylake, William Martin, coxswain of the New Brighton lifeboat, was interviewed with regard to a statement made by William Bramhall of the Liverpool No.2 boat to the effect that the New Brighton boat *Henry Richardson* was within hailing distance of the capsized lifeboat, but that they went straight on to the *Maxwell*, taking no notice of the plight of the Liverpool boat.

Martin said in reply that owing to the fury of the gale and the darkness of the night, no one could see the Liverpool boat, or hear the cries for assistance. The New Brighton lifeboatmen very much regretted that they were quite unaware of the distress of the Liverpool lifeboat's crew.

75

That same evening, arrangements for the funeral of the three lifeboatmen were, by direction of the Dock Board and with the consent of the next-of-kin, entrusted to the Liverpool Watermen`s Sailing Club (LWSC), of which all three men had been members. The LWSC placed the responsibility for the arrangements into the hands of a sub-committee consisting of Nicholas F. Conway, James Moore and R. Stuart.

The subcommittee met and then informed Mr. Joseph Bennett the honorary secretary of the LWSC, that they had decided on a public funeral, to take place on Sunday July 24th provided the inquest on Emmanuel Rodriguez was completed before that date.

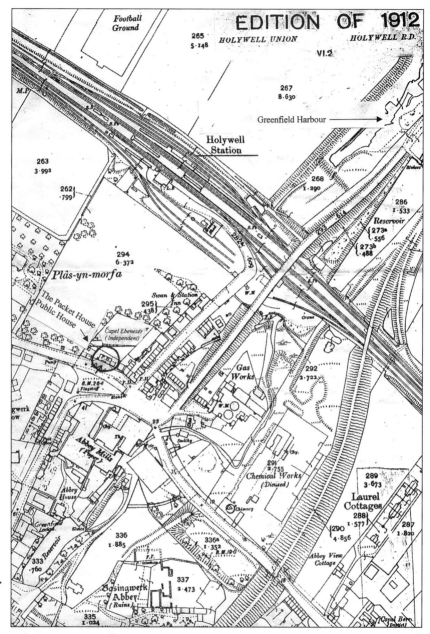

Ordnance map of the Greenfields area, Holywell, showing the Packet House Public House and Greenfield Harbour.

Notes:-

1.The present Dock Company building at the pierhead (formerly Mann Island) was the first of the three buildings to be constructed (the Liver and Cunard buildings) and was officially opened in 1907 by Robert Gladstone, then Chairman of the Board. The Liver building was opened in 1911 and the Cunard building in 1916.

2. James de Bels Adam was elected to office on 9 November 1891.

3. A steam flat was the steam powered version of the sailing weaver flat; basically a small and simple steam coaster, mainly built by firms such as Yarwoods.

Chapter Six

The Lifeboatmen come home

A ll three men lost from the Liverpool No. 2 lifeboat were Roman Catholics. It had been decided they would be interred together at the Roman Catholic cemetery at Ford, Liverpool. If the inquest on Rodriguez did not take place until Monday 25th July then the interment would take place the following day.

Mr. Bennett was then instructed by the committee to hire the band of the boys' training ship HMS *Indefatigable* [1] which was then permanently moored in the River Mersey off Rock Ferry, to invite the coxswain and crew of the New Brighton lifeboat, the crews of the Liverpool lifeboats, the survivors of the *Maxwell*, the members of the Watermen's Society and all relations, friends and sympathisers.

Messrs. R. McDougall & Company, undertakers, of Renshaw

Street, Liverpool, were requested to carry out the interment, acting upon the instructions of the LWSC.

This included the conveyance of the bodies to Liverpool. The bodies of Morgan and Ruffler could be transferred to Liverpool as soon as Mr. McDougall had made the necessary arrangements. He had also been instructed that in the likely event of the Coroner holding the inquest on Emmanuel Rodriguez on either Friday night, July 22nd or Saturday morning July 23rd, he must make sure that the body was brought to Liverpool immediately so that the funeral could take place as planned on July 24th. In this eventuality the funeral procession would start from the open space opposite St. Nicholas church at one o'clock.

That night, the Flintshire Coroner William Davies held the inquest on Emmanuel Rodriguez at the Packet House, Greenfield, Flintshire. Mrs. Julia Ann Rodriguez of 40 Maghull Street, Liverpool, identified the body as that of her late husband Emmanuel. William Bramhall of Denison Street, Liverpool, one of the survivors of the capsized lifeboat and Captain William F. Jones of the steam flat *John* were called on to give evidence. The jury returned a verdict of accidental drowning. With the inquests completed and the verdicts given, the bodies of the three Liverpool lifeboatmen were released to the undertakers.

Work on salvaging the *Maxwell* had progressed rapidly throughout all that day and by late afternoon the Liverpool Salvage Association stated that they would attempt to raise her the following day, Saturday 23rd July if the weather was favourable. That night the captain of the *Alert* was instructed to take up a position in the embayment[2] between the George's and Prince's landing stages in case the *Alert's* services should he required to tow out the lifeboat, or to render any other service incidental to the navigation of the river. She had steam up and was fully lighted in accordance with the regulations provided for vessels going to sea. The *Alert* was ready for any emergency that might arise.

Early on Saturday morning Lieutenant Simpson RN, Water

Bailiff for the MDHB went out to the wreck with four of the Liverpool Steam Tug Company's powerful tugs. The rents in the *Maxwell's* hull below the water line had by now been plugged as tight as possible with oakum and enough of her cargo had been moved to allow the large steam pumps which had been put aboard by the LSA to operate. The weather was favourable and with the tugs standing by, the order to commence pumping was given. The intention was to pump the *Maxwell* out and then tow her off the bank at high water, keeping her afloat by continuous pumping until she could be got up river to a safe berth.

After pumping flat out for some time the operation was temporarily suspended owing to the breakdown of one of the pumps. With time and tide against then it became obvious that they would not now be able to discharge enough water from her holds prior to high water, to enable them to float her. Reluctantly the order to stop the pumps was given, and Lt. Simpson returned to Liverpool. The salvage men would resume their efforts later that day with the coming of the next tide.

That Saturday morning whilst the men of the LSA were toiling to bring the remains of the *Maxwell* back to life, Messrs. McDougall were making arrangements to have the remains of the three lifeboatmen transferred to Liverpool in readiness for the funeral the following day. The body of Emmanuel Rodriguez was brought, enclosed in a polished oak coffin with massive brass fittings, from the Packet House. As the coffin was moved from Greenfields a Mrs. Davies of Marsh Cottage, Greenfields, placed a beautiful wreath - the work of her own hands - on the coffin, saying she herself had a son who was a sailor. The coffin and its cortege, on reaching the railway station boarded the 10.50 express to Liverpool. Daniel Morgan's remains were brought to Liverpool from the cottage hospital at Hoylake and the body of William Ruffler, the youngest of the three, was brought from the Leasowe mortuary, all the deceased being enclosed in coffins of a similar pattern, supplied by McDougall's.

At about the same time that the coffins arrived in Liverpool the Water Bailiff was once again leaving the Liverpool landing stage for the wreck of the *Maxwell*. On arrival, Lt. Simpson was informed that all the steam pumps were functioning correctly and the pumping operation had recommenced. Captain Young proposed to keep the steam pumps going non-stop right over the slack water period and on to high tide with the hope that by then the *Maxwell* would be buoyant enough to be hauled off.

It was noted by an observer on that day that from the appearance of the Lord Mayor's collecting box outside the Town Hall, the public had made a ready response to his worship's appeal. A goodly number of half-crowns, florins, shillings, sixpences and coppers had already been contributed. Mrs. Simpson, the proprietor of Simpson's Tea Rooms offered to place a bowl on the landing stage for the benefit of the sufferers, but the Marine Committee of the MDHB did not see their way to sanctioning this proposal.

The MDHB let it be known that they would look to the welfare of the widows and orphans. In the days that followed this statement was to mislead many into not contributing to the fund and it was probably owing to this resolve that the placing of Mrs. Simpson's bowl on the landing stage had been discouraged. Another fund raising scheme launched that same day in response to the Lord Mayor's appeal was the idea of a Mr. William Cox of 36 Manchester Street, Liverpool. Mr. Cox, a naturalist, offered a handsome case of preserved birds to be drawn for. The case, put on display at his shop door, measured 3ft. 8in. x 2ft. 4in. x 1ft. 4in. and contained a pair of herons, a pair of solitary snipe and a pair of jacksnipe. The prize was valued at about £10 and in order that the working classes might have an opportunity of participating in the draw, the tickets were sold at two pence each and would remain on sale for ten days.

John Hughes, who had been admitted to the Northern Hospital on the morning of the disaster, was released that

Saturday, leaving only Charles Norton and John Gavin in hospital.

Mr. Joseph Bennett, honorary secretary of the Liverpool Watermen`s Sailing Club, and Mr. S.S. Chiswell, secretary to McDougall`s the undertakers spent Saturday morning completing the funeral arrangements. A plot had been acquired at Ford cemetery by Mr. Nicholas Conway of the LWSC in which the three men would be interred. Arrangements complete, the LWSC announced to the general public that the funeral would take place the following day, Sunday July 24th and would start from the low water bridge at the pier head at one o'clock.

It was also announced that day that a collection limited to five shillings or under, had realised £70 to £80. The widows of the disaster victims were at once given a considerable proportion of this amount to help meet their immediate requirements. That afternoon Captain Fraser again returned to the *Maxwell* and found salvage operations well advanced, the steam pumps working to capacity and discharging great volumes of water from the holds. There were many tugs, tenders and other vessels in attendance, their crews and all others involved in the salvage operation, be it salvage men, divers, seamen, riggers, or galley boys all waiting in eager anticipation for high water - the signal for success or failure.

As the tide rose it became evident that the pumps were mastering the now greatly reduced inflow of water into the holds. Several of the tugs now moved in on the wreck and, towing lines were secured to her stern and quarters. The remainder of the great paddle tugs lay off in readiness to tend her if she pulled clear of the bank that held her so firmly. As high water approached, the tugboats, taking up the slack on their massive hawsers, began to take the strain.

At high water the signal to haul away was given and with one mightily combined effort the tugs, paddles churning the sea into a froth, hauled the sailing ship off the sandbank that for the past four days had threatened to become her grave. This victory was greeted with jubilant cheering and applause and the shrieking of sirens from the attendant vessels. Once clear of the bank and in deeper water the paddle tugs took up their designated positions around the *Maxwell* and slowly guided her back towards Liverpool. With the steam pumps kept going and the remainder of her cargo of coal being trimmed as she went, the ship was successfully righted. That evening the *Maxwell* was once again in the River Mersey.

Crowds of sightseers had gathered on the Wallasey side of the river to witness the crippled vessel`s progress. Assisted by five tugs the *Maxwell* was manoeuvred into Alfred Dock, Birkenhead where Captain Fraser was put in charge of her.

The discharging of her cargo would go ahead day and night until complete. The steam pumps were kept going all the time she was alongside, with the salvage company`s engineers in charge of the pumping operations. While the *Maxwell* remained in Alfred dock, Captain Fraser took up lodgings in the Seacombe Hotel, a short distance from the *Maxwell*`s berth.

From early Sunday morning, crowds of people from both sides of the River Mersey began to converge on the pier head. Liverpool was about to witness a truly remarkable display of public sympathy with the relatives of those who had lost their lives in the disaster, the likes of which had rarely been seen in the city before or since.

The band of the Boys` Training Ship *Indefatigable* had been brought ashore by the steam paddle tug *Commodore* that had been placed at the service of the Liverpool Watermen`s Sailing Club for that purpose by the tugboat owner Mr. Jolliffe. Once ashore the band formed up and marched from the landing stage to the Pier head, taking up a position at the head of the cortege opposite St. Nicholas Church from the belfry of which was rung a continuous muffled peel that brought a very sombre feeling to the gathering.

H.M.S. Indefatigable.

A 50 gun frigate launched in 1844 by King William IV.

Used as a seamanship training school for boys, moored in the River Mersey off Rock ferry from about 1870 to 1914.

The Indefatigable band led the funeral procession of the Liverpool lifeboatmen on Sunday July 24th 1892.

By this time the crowds had become immense, and the churchyard, pier head walls and all other elevated positions were occupied by hundreds of people eager to see the funeral procession. As the cortege began to form shortly before one o'clock, a passage through the dense crowd was kept by the river police for the hearses and coaches. The procession, comprising as it did three funerals, was unusually long; the task of marshalling it, amid so many people, was not easy.

However, directed by Mr. S.S. Chiswell of McDougall`s, the funeral procession started shortly after one o'clock in this order: first the hearse containing the remains of Emmanuel Rodriguez, followed by three carriages containing his family and friends, secondly the hearse which bore Daniel Morgan followed by three carriages and thirdly the hearse bearing the body of William Ruffler and three carriages of private mourners.

There followed a long line of nine carriages with the survivors of the Liverpool No.2 lifeboat's crew, officers of the Liverpool Watermen`s Sailing Club... committee members, officers and representatives of the MDHB, the survivors of the sailing ship *Maxwell* and others, a four horse Wagonette with the New Brighton lifeboat crew and finally a long procession of conveyances containing some 200 members of the Liverpool Watermen`s Sailing Club and general mourners.

The coffins bore many wreaths and floral tributes from families and friends, and others were to arrive; from Hoylake wreaths were sent bearing the inscription 'with sincere sympathy from Captain Whiteway of Hoylake` while one for each of the coffins was sent by the committee of the LWSC. Lt. Belam RN placed a wreath on each coffin on behalf of the MDHB. There were also floral tributes from Mr. & Mrs. Stuart and Mr. & Mrs Carter of St. Paul`s Square.

The principal mourners for Emmanuel Rodriguez, who was aged 44 years, were Mrs. Julia Ann Rodriguez and her seven children, the youngest being Louisa Rodriguez[3] aged 4 years, together with Mr. & Mrs. Baker (brother in law and sister), Mr. George Rodriguez (brother), Mrs Boothroyd (sister), Mr J Boothroyd, Mr Edwin Boothroyd and Miss Boothroyd (nephews & niece), Mr Herratty, Mr R Shaw, Mr & Mrs Carter, Mr & Mrs Baker Mr Fisher and Mr Tully.

Among the relatives and friends of Daniel Morgan present were his widow and her three children, Miss Ellis (cousin), Mrs Stuart (aunt), Mr J Foster, Mr & Mrs W Stuart, Mrs R Stuart, Mr Bartley (all cousins) and Mr Hasall (nephew). Daniel Morgan was aged 45 years.

The family and friends of Ruffler, aged 41 years, included his widow and her five children, Mr Ruffler (brother), Mrs Smith and Mrs Doran (sisters in law), Mrs McDonald (daughter), Mr & Mrs George Wilson (brother in law and sister), Mrs Ruffler (mother), Miss Ruffler (sister) and Miss Ruffler (cousin).

The surviving members of the Liverpool lifeboat's crew present were Coxswain Nicholas Hinchley, Albert Martin, John Hughes, William Ellison, Henry Beaver, David Thomas and William Bramhall. The two other members of the crew, Charles Norton and John Gavin were still detained in hospital on the day of the funeral.

The New Brighton lifeboatmen who attended were Coxswain William Martin, George Robinson (2nd Coxswain), W Jones (1st Coxswain), W. Jones (2nd Coxswain), Samuel Jones, John Sourberry, William Batty, Thomas Jones, J. Rogers, John Fairclough, H. Gribbins, J. Goss, J. Evans, Charles McDonald, Nathaniel Linacker, W J Liverage, J.Gribbins, George Morris, Alfred Wylle and Charles Eddington.

The Liverpool Watermen's Sailing Club were represented by Messrs. Nicholas F. Conway, Robert Stuart, T. Cooke, J. Moore, R. Bennet and J Ryan, members of the committee and honorary officers. Lt. Sweny RN, Marine Surveyor and Lieutenant Belam RN were present on behalf of the Dock Board.

List of crewmembers from the Liverpool No. 2 Lifeboat
July 19th 1892.

Nicholas Hinchley (Coxswain)
Emmanuel Rodriguez (Dead)
William Ruffler (Dead)
Daniel Morgan (Dead)
William Bramhall (Injured)
John Gannon (Injured)
John Gavin (Injured)
Albert Martin (Injured)
Charles Norton (Injured)
John Hughes (Injured)
William Ellison
David Thomas
Henry Beaver

Heaven protect those brave men
That venture on the wave
In the hour of danger
Their fellow men to save.
Let's hope they're with the angels
Resting peaceful evermore.
God will protect the loved ones
They have left behind on shore.

88

That Sunday morning the people of Liverpool and many from the other side of the River Mersey, turned out in their thousands to view the funeral procession as it moved towards the place of interment. A stranger, seeing the masses of people tramping through the main arteries of the city and the chief thoroughfares leading from the Heights of Everton, all making for the pier head, would have imagined that some event of great moment was about to take place.

One eye witness observed that :

'*Here among the immense throng of people could be seen the respectably dressed man and his wife, there the crudely shod and poorly clad labourer, while the numbers of basket women and the innumerable hosts of the great unwashed were exceedingly large, and although the lower orders of the city were very much in evidence, the presence and efforts of the large body of police spread along the whole line of the route were hardly needed.*'

Although no doubt many of the people who lined the route were merely spectators, yet there prevailed in the hearts of thousands a warm feeling of sympathy for the unhappy participants in this sad ceremony. This was evident by the conduct and reverential attitude of the people.

The funeral procession headed by the *Indefatigable*'s band playing 'The dead march in Saul`, proceeded at walking pace from St. Nicholas Church, her bells still tolling, and moved slowly up Chapel Street. All along Tithebarn Street, Great Crosshall Street and Byrom Street, as the cortege slowly made its way towards Scotland Road, it was greeted with loud expressions of pity for the relatives of the deceased by the women in the crowd, while the men uncovered their heads as the hearses went by. On all sides along the whole crowded route to the cemetery the same sympathetic feeling prevailed, while from time to time both men and women alike, strangers to the dead lifeboatmen, could be seen wiping their eyes.

On reaching the lower end of Scotland Road the appearance of the streets was most remarkable. As far as the eye could see was a sea of faces, while hundreds of shop windows were occupied by residents, even the lamp posts were engaged by young urchins wanting to see over the heads of the crowd.

Through Stanley Road and Litherland Road similar masses of people were congregated. On reaching Bank Hall the band was transferred to a conveyance and the cortege moved forward more briskly, scores of young men and women keeping pace with the coaches. The entrance to the cemetery chapel at Ford was almost blocked by the crowds who had accompanied the funeral on foot, and it was as much as the chief mourners could do to get into the edifice, which was already crowded and echoing with a chorus of lamentation, above which could be heard at intervals the chanting of the robed priest, the Reverend Father Browne.

The sorrowful service, conducted amid so much added misery, was brief. At its close the remains of the three men were borne across the cemetery to a grave situated beneath a bank at some distance from the church, with Father Browne leading the way. The crowds swarmed round on every side, running on ahead and surging up the bank, eager to view the last solemn ritual with which the bodies of the lifeboat heroes were lowered to their final resting place. The *Indefatigable* boys then sang the hymn 'Days and moments quickly flying', their clear voices rising above the buzz of the crowds, who seemed visibly awed by the service. With the funeral ended the people poured out of the several gates of the cemetery and streamed back along the road to Liverpool, accompanied by the coaches and cabs of the mourners.

The day of the funeral also saw large numbers of people at the Alfred Dock, Birkenhead, to see the sailing ship *Maxwell* at her berth.

At about 5.30 in the evening Ellen Gilfoyle, a ten-year-old girl of 16 Back St. Anne Street Liverpool, accidentally slipped from the quay into the dock. Samuel Hatton, Captain of the steam flat

Mary Helen which lay nearby, quickly seized a rope and without hesitation jumped in after the child. Both of them were hauled out of the water in a few moments by PC 109 Bebington and a number of other men. Apart from getting wet Ellen did not seem to be any the worse for her adventure and was duly allowed to go home. Two days after this incident Captain Hatton was awarded 20 shillings by the Liverpool Shipwreck and Humane Society for his prompt action in saving the child.

That Sunday evening although it was very hot, Pembroke Chapel was more crowded than on any wintry Sunday night when popular subjects were discussed by the eloquent pastor, the Reverend C.F. Aked. The aisles were packed, the upper galleries filled, and latecomers had to content themselves with seats behind the platform upon the Baptistery.

The great congregation was deeply moved throughout the discourse; during the opening description of the lifeboat disaster a breathless silence prevailed. Mr. Aked took for his text John XV, 13 *'Greater love hath no man than this, that a man lay down his life for his friends'.* He went on to say that these lifeboatmen had gone beyond that. They had given an extension to the idea of friendship and had cheerfully laid down their lives for those who were no friends of theirs.

After a thrilling description of the scene, the Rev. Aked said that it was time that the lifeboat service was taken out of the hands of private philanthropy and public beneficence and made a charge upon the nation, adding that it was just as much a nation's business to provide adequate and efficient lifeboats as to provide lighthouses. Mr. Aked then sketched out to the crowd the rise and progress and varied fortunes of the Lifeboat Institution and dealt in glowing terms upon the heroism written large upon the pages of its history. At the conclusion of this tense and emotional service a collection was made for the widows and orphans of the dead lifeboatmen, which amounted to £28.8d.6d.

On Monday July 25th 1892 at a meeting of underwriters, Mr.

91

Rundell the Liverpool Salvage Association's representative, received instructions to pay the MDHB all expenses incurred in connection with the *Maxwell* and her cargo.

The last of her cargo having been discharged the hold was swept clean and the leaks stopped by lavish use of cement. The steam pumps were taken away and an examination made of the damage sustained from the inside. This was quite considerable, with one hundred and twenty six floor frames and reverse frames on the port side and forty on the starboard side broken. The rudder had sheared close to the closing plate and the sternpost from the second pintle, also the plates from the sternpost in a line to some 15 feet along the keel were broken and buckled. Fortunately for the *Maxwell* the after run of the ship had been constructed with large pockets starting from a 20 foot base filled with cement, built up and decreasing in size as far as the tween decks.

When she had grounded, the cement in great measure held in place, which greatly reduced the inflow of water; this in turn, after the rents had been plugged with oakum, enabled the steam pumps to deal with the water still entering the holds and made it possible to save her. After her internal examination the *Maxwell* was moved into dry dock in the Great Float, Birkenhead where she remained for several days while the Lloyds surveyors, shipbuilders and other interested parties examined her and estimated the cost of repairs.

That day, Charles Norton was discharged from the Liverpool Northern hospital, leaving John Gavin the only remaining survivor still detained in hospital. The following day Tuesday July 26th - a cartload of gear and equipment belonging to the No. 2 lifeboat which had been picked up off the Welsh coast, was brought to the Liverpool landing stage where Mr. King, master of the Prince's landing stage had it stowed in the boathouse. Amongst the items recovered were the lifeboat's mast, sails, oars and tiller, oilskins, jackets, leggings, sou'westers and lifebelts. It was a sad reminder, to those who witnessed the transportation and stowing of the equipment, of the tragic events of that terrible night only one short week before. On a more cheerful note, that day John Gavin was allowed home from the cottage hospital, Hoylake, although it was to be some time before the injury to his knee would allow him to resume his duties. The next day all the survivors of the No. 2 boat were sent to a village near Wrexham by the MDHB in order to recuperate their health.

The lifeboatmen were provided with all necessities at the expense of the Dock Board, and furnished with pocket money, in order that they might enjoy themselves.

Notes:-

1.H.M.S. *Indefatigable,* a 50 gun frigate, was launched in 1844 by King William IV. In 1864 John Clint, Liverpool seaman and ship owner, founded a school to train boys as seamen to serve in the fleets of Liverpool merchant ships. The Admiralty loaned the vessel and the Liverpool ship owning family Bibby had her converted into a floating boarding school. She was moored off Rock Ferry in the River Mersey and served until 1914 when, again thanks to the Bibby family, she was replaced by H.M.S. *Phaeton,* one of the last Royal Navy ships to use both sail and engines. She retained the name *Indefatigable.*

2. A recess set back from the faces of the main quay. To enclose in a bay .

3. 46 years later, almost to the day, Louisa became my grandmother. Great grandmother Julia Ann died in 1935 aged 84 years. Louisa died in 1967 at the age of 76. Both are buried at Ford Cemetery, Liverpool.

Chapter Seven

Aftermath of a disaster

O n the day that the lifeboatmen set off to convalesce, Mr. Joseph Bennett, honorary secretary of the Liverpool Watermen's Sailing Club wrote to a local newspaper, making reference to a paragraph which had appeared in the same paper a few days earlier. The paragraph referred to the lifeboat disaster and included the words *The Board (Dock) has also let it be known that they will look after the future welfare of the widows and orphans.* '

Mr. Bennett wrote:

This statement has, not unreasonably I think, been understood by many of your readers to mean that the MDHB have announced that they will undertake to provide for the future of the widows and orphans of the unfortunate lifeboatmen. This has discouraged many charitably-disposed

95

persons who would, but for the misleading statement, have freely contributed to the fund being raised for the benefit of the widows and orphans now left totally un-provided for.'

Mr. Bennett continued by stating:

'I am authorised to deny that the Dock Board has in any way intimated their intention of doing as your report states. No doubt the Board will do something, but all the money that can possibly be raised will be needed if the families of the three brave fellows who lost their lives when nobly doing their duty on July 20th are to be kept from starvation. Trusting you will give the same prominence to this as you have done to the statement referred to.

Editorial comments in the Merseyside press at the time lent support to this view:-

There are the families of the drowned sailors to be provided for, they lost their lives as much for patriotic duty as if they had died in battle.

Let it not be said that the wives and families of men at our own door, who lost their lives in discharging the noblest duty that can devolve upon mankind, have had their cup of misery added to by the cold neglect of those who have the means to help.

During the course of that same day, the MDHB having been fully compensated for all their charges and expenses allowed Messrs. Johnston & Sproule, owners of the *Maxwell*, to take possession of the vessel and her cargo. The owners then instructed Captain Fraser to have the ship made ready to be taken across the river for repair by T. Royden & Sons, her builders.

Using more cement to cork the leaks and taking all precautions for a safe passage across the river, Captain Fraser had a team of riggers sent on board and the *Maxwell* left dry dock and was towed to Alfred Basin, there to wait for the lock gates to open allowing access to the river. Captain Fraser later recalled that 'Just on the point of leaving the basin, a red-faced old chap in broadcloth and a silk hat came aboard in a great state of excitement.` This gentleman handed Captain Fraser a note instructing him to hand over the ship to a representative of Clover & Clayton, ship repairers of Birkenhead. This Captain Fraser did. [1]

Mr. Gregory, clerk to Johnston & Sproule explained that the reason for such a change in the ship`s disposal was that Mr. Sproule had agreed to a deal worked out by Mr. Wallace of the underwriters whereby the underwriters would sell the *Maxwell* to Clover & Clayton, a transaction which would largely benefit the underwriters. They in turn would pay Mr. Sproule the full insurance on the *Maxwell*, and so the ship changed ownership, but only briefly. After an extensive overhaul and refit in the Clover & Clayton yard in Birkenhead, she was sold to the Liverpool ship owners Nicholas & McGill. She remained under their flag for two years, and then in 1894 she was sold to John Edgar & Company, also of Liverpool.

On 1st April 1902 while on passage from San Francisco to Hull, the *Maxwell* was in collision with the German steam ship *Patagonia* (3,016 tons) of the Hamburg-Amerika Line, and sunk off Dungeness. Once again her crew were saved but this time the sailing ship *Maxwell* was to be lost forever.

On Thursday July 28th the crew of the New Brighton lifeboat *Henry Richardson* received a present of a pound a man from the owners of the *Maxwell*. The lifeboatmen wished to publicly acknowledge the kindness of the owners and sent for publication this letter:-

The Lifeboathouse,

New Brighton

28 July 1892.

Messrs. Johnston & Sproule,

26 Old Hall Street, Liverpool.

Gentlemen,

we the crew of the New Brighton lifeboat Henry Richardson that on the night of the 19th July 1892 rescued the captain and crew of the ship Maxwell wish to thank you for your present, not only for its amount, a sovereign to each of the crew being sufficient to be appreciated for its own sake, but also as an acknowledgement of a service that was really severe though only what we are prepared to again attempt whenever it shall be necessary.

We are gentlemen, yours most respectfully.

Here the letter was signed by all sixteen crewmembers.

A special meeting of the committee for the Marine Department of the MDHC was held on July 28th, attended by Mr. James Baron, the chairman, Mr. Robert G. Allen, Mr. Benson Rathbone, Mr. Reginald Bushell and Mr. John Branker. The committee having investigated all the circumstances in connection with the capsizing of the Liverpool No. 2 lifeboat, it was resolved that the No. 2 lifeboat had been used on many former occasions in heavy weather, she had never before capsized and her crew had entire confidence in her.

As to the question whether a tug should not have been engaged when the lifeboat's crew were mustered, to tow the lifeboat out in case of need, on this the committee noted that no difficulty had been experienced on any former occasion in obtaining the immediate services of a tug when required.

The committee recommended to the Board that a sum of £100 be granted, to be applied during the ensuing twelve months in weekly payments, for the benefit of the widows and orphans in proportion to the numbers of the respective families and that the question of a further grant for the purpose indicated, be considered at the end of the period stated. It was also recommended that a sum of £30 be equally divided amongst the ten survivors of the crew of the lifeboat.

It was further resolved to recommend that a donation of £10 be made to the Hoylake cottage hospital. All the recommendations put forward by the committee for the Marine Department were adopted by the MDHC, including one submitted on August 8th which requested that the Marine Surveyor. Lt. Sweny be authorised to arrange for the articles of clothing lost by the crew of the No. 2 boat on the night of the tragedy to be replaced by the Board, also that a final payment of £3 be made to each of the survivors, except John Gavin who suffered a knee injury when the lifeboat capsized, to whom an additional sum of 13/- per week be paid for a period to be determined at the discretion of the Marine Surveyor.

In the weeks following the lifeboat disaster, people from in and around the city of Liverpool continued to contribute to the appeal fund. On August 8th, the day that the MDHB agreed to make their final payment to the surviving members of the crew, the Waterloo and District Cycling Club held a fancy dress carnival to raise money for the appeal fund. The event was arranged by the committees assisted by Mr. J. Richardson Mr. R.S. Rowlinson and Mr. W. Routledge as joint secretaries with Mr. B. Attwood Beaver as Treasurer.

The cyclists set off at 7.30 p.m. from Marine Crescent, Waterloo and proceeded along Wellington Street, Oxford Road, Brighton-le-Sands, over the railway bridge along College Road, Crosby Road, Church Road Seaforth, Sandy Road, Claremont Road, Crosby Road and South Road, back to the starting point, collecting along the way. On August 16th Mr. Cox the Manchester Street naturalist held the draw for the case of preserved birds. In the course of ten days 6,500 tickets had been sold at two pence per ticket.

The draw for the prize was made at Manchester Street in the presence of two representatives of the Liverpool newspapers, while Mr. Francis Bradburne of Baines Place, Breck Road, and Mr. Wilson of the Clock Hotel, West Derby Road, officiated. The prize was won by Mr. Slocomb of 56 Warbreck Road, Walton, and Mr. Cox was able to hand to the Lord Mayor's secretary the sum of £30 towards the appeal fund, while Mr. Attwood Beaver of the Waterloo and District Cycling Club was able to announce that the fancy dress carnival had raised £125. *2*

Soon after the events of July 1892 the MDHB began to realise that it was becoming increasingly difficult to maintain the lifeboat service to the high standard expected of them. The officers of the Board were hard pressed and occupied by many other duties so that the lifeboat service was gradually neglected. Under increasing criticism from the press and other bodies highlighting the shortcomings in the lifeboat service, the MDHB began to listen to the suggestions made to them through the local committee of the Liverpool and New Brighton branch of the Royal National Lifeboat Institution, that the Institution should take over their lifeboat service and manage it for them. At the annual meeting of the branch held in February 1894 it was proposed by Mr. James Samuelson that a sub-committee should be appointed to negotiate with the Docks Board in the matter.

This suggestion was at once adopted, and the sub-committee consisting of Admiral Gough, C.B., Mr. Harold D. Bateson, Mr.

Francis Henderson and Mr. C.H. Beloe, Captain Blennerhasset and Mr. Eustace Stacy, set to work in earnest to bring about the suggested transfer. After careful consultation between the Docks Board authorities and the Royal National Lifeboat Institution's Liverpool and New Brighton committee, an agreement was eventually reached.

As pointed out at the beginning of this story, part of the agreement was that the MDHB would donate an annual sum of money to the RNLI, and that of the five lifeboat stations then under the control of the MDHB four would come under the control of the RNLI and the one at the Liverpool landing stage would be abolished. The eventual success of the negotiations were due in no small way to the tact and energy of Mr. Harold D. Bateson, a well known Liverpool solicitor, and Honorary Secretary of the Liverpool branch. Mr. Bateson threw himself heart and soul into the matter and, being well backed up by the committees in Liverpool and London, carried the negotiations successfully through.

On July lst 1894 without any fuss or ceremony the transfer was made and the Liverpool Lifeboat Service was no more.

Notes:-

1.Shortly after being relieved of his command Captain Fraser, after an interview with representatives of Messrs. Johnston & Sproule, agreed to put over £2,000 into a new ship they proposed building. He stayed in Cumberland for a time, visiting the Naval Architect who was responsible for the design of the ship in Liverpool from time to time.The *Maxwell* was to be Captain Fraser's last command, and after 27 years at sea he became Marine Superintendent for Messrs. Johnston & Sproule.

Captain Thomas Garry Fraser was born at Harrington, Cumberland in 1850. He first went to sea in 1865, gaining his Master's ticket at the age of 22. He completed 25 voyages before leaving the sea. He died in 1934 and is buried in Harrington churchyard.

2. I have during my research investigated every possible source available to me in attempting to establish just how much the Lord Mayor's appeal fund actually raised and how the money was eventually distributed, but unfortunately without success.

Epilogue

Full Circle

At the beginning of November 1986, after numerous telephone enquiries and many personal visits to Ford cemetery, Liverpool, in my endeavours to find the grave of my great grandfather, and as my research into the Liverpool Lifeboat disaster produced more information, I was at last able to give Elizabeth Nelson, the Registrar at the cemetery, a date enabling her to find the exact date of the funeral and also the number of the grave. But it was to take a while longer before the actual grave was found.

It took Miss Nelson some time to find the plans showing the layout of the graves for that period, and when found, what a poor state of repair they were in. They also appeared to be not quite accurate as the numbers on the backs of the gravestones still standing did not correspond with those on the plan.

However, the staff at Ford Lodge, after scrutinising the back of numerous headstones, many crumbled and corroded with time, at last found the number sequence they had been seeking. Soon after, I received a letter dated November 21st 1986 from Elizabeth Nelson, informing me that the grave had been found.

Seventeen years had now elapsed since my late uncle Tony and I had first tried to find the grave. Instead of feeling elated at the news I felt strangely subdued and became rather reluctant to visit the gravesite. As my research into the story became more involved, the people and events surrounding the disaster had become very much alive to me, now with the finding of the grave it was as though I had just been given confirmation of the death of a friend and I did not want to accept the fact. However, in February 1987 I made arrangements with Miss Nelson to be shown the grave.

On arrival at Ford Lodge I was first shown the interment book for 1892, which confirmed the date of burial, and I was much surprised to find that all three lifeboatmen had been buried in the same grave. I was then taken by a member of the staff to the site of the grave and was very saddened to find that the burial place of the three Liverpool lifeboatmen now lay unmarked, which of course was why Tony and I had been unable to find it. Any monument or stone that had been erected to the memory of those brave men had been vandalised and long since removed, as had so many other memorial stones in this sad place.

The now unmarked grave of the Liverpool lifeboatmen Emmanuel Rodriguez (the author's great grandfather) aged 44 years, Daniel Morgan aged 45 years and William Ruffler aged 41 years.

First seen by the author in February 1987 at Ford cemetery, Liverpool.

105

H aving led me to the site, my escort then left me with my thoughts. I spent quite some time at the graveside picturing in my mind's eye the events that had brought the three lifeboatmen to this their final resting place, then having paid my respects to their memory, I crossed to the bank where nearly a hundred years before, the crowds had surged up to gain a better view of the last solemn ritual of the funeral service.

Now all that stood on the bank, besides a few weary-looking trees, were several groups of wild daffodils, their heads bowed against the wind. I picked just one and laid it on the lifeboatmen's grave, then having gathered my thoughts I took some photographs of the site. Out of curiosity I decided to read some of the inscriptions on the headstones nearby. The one to the right was so small that I had to lie on my stomach to read the wording, which was hardly visible. I rubbed away some of the grime, and found the name Julia Ann Rodriguez.

To say I was surprised to find the name 'Rodriguez' on the stone would be, to say the least, an understatement. I wrote down the few brief details given on the stone and returned to Ford Lodge very deep in thought. [1]

Miss Nelson's letter had also informed me that she had found during her search that Mr. Nicholas Conway had owned the lifeboatmen`s grave, and that there is still room in the grave. Mr. Conway, as I was later to discover, had been one of the more prominent members of the Liverpool Watermen's Sailing Club committee and was one of the sub-committee responsible for the funeral arrangements of the lifeboatmen and the acquisition of the gravesite.

My next request to Miss Nelson was to find who now owned the grave. A few weeks later she informed me that no deeds for the grave could be found, and that if I so wished I could claim it. I requested that the necessary arrangements be made.

The grave of my great grandmother Julia Ann Rodriguez, next to my great grandfather's grave.

Julia Ann died in 1935 aged 84 years.

O n May 21st 1987 at Ford Lodge for a fee of £10 I signed a document, witnessed and signed by Miss Nelson, declaring that I was now the owner of the Liverpool lifeboatmen's grave. I intend some time in the not too distant future to erect a memorial to the proud memory of the three long-forgotten men, and to use in its construction sand taken from Burbo Bank and Leasowe foreshore near to the Leasowe lighthouse (which still stands), and stone from the Flintshire coast.

I think probably the most fitting tribute to the lifeboatmen of that bygone age came from the late Captain Richard England when, in his excellent book *Schooner Man* he makes reference to the service of the Moelfre and Anglesey sailing and pulling lifeboat *Charles & Eliza Laura* to the schooner *Excel* on the 28th October 1927.

Captain England wrote:

'During the course of a lifetime I have witnessed many acts of gallantry both afloat and ashore, but for sheer unselfish heroism I award first place to the men who manned the open sailing and pulling lifeboats.

To pull or sail out to sea in a raging gale, unable to communicate with the shore and depending solely on their own skill, strength and endurance for survival, all in the hopes of saving lives, required a special breed of men.'

Opposite Page: The document passing ownership of the Liverpool lifeboatmen's grave to the author.

108

City of Liverpool, in the County ⎱ To Wit
Palatine of Lancaster. ⎰

I, JAMES. ANTHONY SULLIVAN. x   of
195. PRINCESS. DR. WEST DERBY LPOOL. R.
                                        do solemnly
and sincerely declare that I am the owner of Grave numbered 68 in Section M.
situated in the Liverpool Catholic Cemetery at   Ford.   of which the deed
is lost and after a diligent search cannot be found.

1892 July 24 - Daniel Morgan - aged 45 years.

1892 July 24 - William Rufler - aged 41 years

1892 July 24 - Emanuel Rodriguez - aged 44 years

"All the above men were drowned by the upsetting
of the Lifeboat outside the Bar." (extract from interment
                                    book of that date)

And I make this solemn Declaration, conscientiously believing the same to
be true, and by virtue of the provisions of the Statutory Declarations Act, 1835.

The above Declaration was solemnly made and subscribed by   Liverpool Catholic Cemeteries
the said   [signature]   .   "FORD LODGE"
                                    at Liverpool aforesaid   Gorsey Lane,
this 21st day of MAY   Ford, L21 0DL.
One thousand nine hundred 87.
                Before me,
              Elizabeth Nelson
                  [Registrar]

Notes

1. Once again as my research into the lifeboat disaster deepened, and I eventually read the Coroner's report into the death of my great grandfather, it was confirmed that my great grandmother was named Julia Ann, she having been called to identify her husband's body.

She died in 1935 and was buried next to Emmanuel Rodriguez 43 years after .

Jim Sullivan October 2001

LIVERPOOL LIFEBOAT DISASTER
ACKNOWLEDGEMENTS
'Storm in the Mersey` by S. Walters
The Liverpool landing stage 1889
The south end of the Liverpool landing stage 1890s
The Atlantic steamer *City of Paris*.
> Courtesy Merseyside Maritime Museum
Vigilant in Albert Dock,1900.
> Courtesy Lancaster Museum
The *Grace Harwar* under sail 1889.
A group photograph maindeck of *Grace Harwar* 1889.
S.S. *Pegu*
> Courtesy the National Maritime Museum.
The Liverpool pilot cutter *George Holt* 1892
Chart of Liverpool Bay 1875
> Courtesy Captain Robinson, Superintendent of Liverpool Pilotage
> (retired)
Rambler
> Courtesy Dr. Dalziel Curator, Lancaster Museum
Plans for the Liverpool lifeboat and the Hoylake lifeboat 1890.
> Courtesy Mr. J.P. Morris, Hon.Archivist Lifeboat
> Enthusiasts Society.
The New Brighton lifeboat Henry Richardson being launched.
> Courtesy Mrs. Shelley Woodroffe, R.N.L.I. Public
> Relations .
Notes on lifeboats
> Courtesy from Mr. G.E. Farr. 'The Tubular Lifeboats
1850-1939'.
The *Mona's Isle III* from Isle of Man Steam Packet Company's postcard
book.
> Courtesy D.H. Deane (Marketing Asst. Isle of Man Steam
Packet Company)
Historical notes *Mona's Isle III*
> Courtesy c/o D.H. Deane, from Mr. Connery, Chappell
Book (Island Lifeline).
Photographs of steam paddle tugs *Great Western* and *Brilliant Star*
> Courtesy Mr. P.N. Thomas, tug boat historian.
Plans and drawings of steam paddle tug *Great Western*

Courtesy from Mr. K. Hinshalwood, M.A., A.L.A.
Librarian, Local History Dept., Renfrew District Council.
Illustration of the steam paddle tender *Vigilant*
    Courtesy 'Port of Liverpool News' (summer 1966) - now
out of circulation.
The steam flats (Weaver) *Madge* & *Bengal*
    Courtesy Mr. R. Middleton, Archivist at the Boat
Museum, Ellesmere Port.
H.M.S. *Indefatigable*
    Courtesy Avid Publications
Extracts from M.D. & H.B. Wreck Book 1892
    Courtesy Captain Roy Williams, M.D. & H.B.
Historical notes on sailing ship *Maxwell*
    Courtesy "Captain Fraser's Voyages" by Marjory Gee.

Other sources of information
Micro Film Unit, Brown-Picton-Hornby Libraries, Liverpool.
Wallasey News' Records Dept., Birkenhead.
Local History Dept. Brown-Picton-Hornb Libraries.
Miss Margaret Evans, Liverpool Maritime Museum, Records Dept.
Dr. A. Scarth, National Museum and Galleries,on Merseyside, Maritime
History Dept.
Records Dept. William Brown Library, Liverpool.
International Library (William Brown Library).
Mr. Read, Chief Archivist, Liverpool Maritime Archives, Islington,
Liverpool.
Mrs. Eccles, Secretary Liverpool Branch World Ship Society.
Mr. G. Sumner, Secretary World Ship Society, Dorset.
Registrar of Ships, Liverpool Customs & Excise (Mr.Dawson.)
Mr. D. Brown, ex coxswain New Brighton Lifeboat.
Mr. J.P. Morris, Hon. Archivist, L.B.E.S.
Alexandra Towing Company, Rae's Ocean Trading, Liverpool Tug
Owners' Assn.
Dept. of Transport, Cardiff.
Registrar of Shipping, Llandaff, Cardiff.
The Harris Library (Local History Dept.), Preston.
Mr. F. Carpenter, Archives Museum, (Photographs), Preston.
Public Record Office, Kew, Richmond, Surrey.

The Registrar General, General Register Office, St. Catherine's House, Kingsway, London.
Liverpool Town Hall, Public Relations Secretary.
Liverpool Sailing Club, Royal Mersey Yacht Club and Hoylake Sailing Club.
Mr. Adrian Ofler, Keeper of Maritime History, Science & Eng. Dept., Heritage Museum, Blandford House, Newcastle.
Mr. Hinchlewood, Chief Historian Local History Dept., Glasgow Museum.
The Sunderland Maritime Museum.
Glasgow University Archives.
Mr. Hoares General Manager Preston Docks.
The Lancashire Records Office, Preston.
The late Mr. Frank Lindstrom, Chief Archivist Cammell Laird Shipyard, Birkenhead.
Silver Marine Shipping Agents, Albany House, Liverpool.
Liverpool Steamship Association, Mann Island, Pier Head, Liverpool.
Miss Ann Harrison, Chief Archivist Manx Museum and National Trust.
Mrs. Nelson, Registrar, Liverpool Catholic Cemetery, Ford, Liverpool.
Mr. Tony Install, Clerical Officer, R.N.L.I.
Lloyds Register of Shipping. (List)
Mrs. Shelley Woodroffe, Public Relations Office, R.N.L.I.
Mr. J.W. Lovegrove, World Ship Society, Liverpool Branch.
Mrs. Clare Sunderland, Picture Editor, Batsford Publishers (B.T. Batsford Ltd.) of London.
Mr. Brian McShane, Surveyor, M.D. & H. Co.
Mr. Hinds, Director of Recreation and Libraries, Borough of Sunderland.
Mrs. Alma Topen, Business Records Collection, University of Glasgow.
Mrs. K. Fletcher, Photographic Dept., Liverpool Museum.
Mr. M.L. Greatbatch, Tyne & Wear Museums Service, Tyneside.
The Merchantile Navy List & Maritime Directory, 1887.
Mr. T. Graham, Central Library, South Tyneside.
The late Mr. C.H. Milsom, Editor "Sea Breezes" magazine.

Bibliography
The Lifeboat - 1894.
The Lifeboat - 1893.
West Coast Shipping by M.K. Stammers
Blow Five by Hallam W.B. (History of the Alexander Towing Co. Ltd.)
The Last Tide by Jack Dakres (History of the Port of Preston.)

Captain Fraser's Voyages 1865-1892 by Mariory Gee.
Schooner Man by Captain Richard England.
History of the Steam Tugs by P.N. Thomas.
The Liverpool Review - 1892.
The Globe - 1892.
The Liverpool Daily Post - 1892 (microfilm.)
The Liverpool Echo - 1892 (microfilm.)
The Annals of Liverpool - 1892.

OTHER PUBLICATIONS AVAILABLE FROM AVID

THETIS - The Admiralty Regrets –The Disaster in Liverpool Bay
by C.Warren & J.Benson

The definitive minute by minute account of this terrible tragedy in 1939 when 99 men lost their lives as HM Submarine *Thetis* undertook her first and only dive. With new photographs and documents as well as a new foreword by a survivors son Derek Arnold, and a new postscript by maritime historian David Roberts. Why didn't anyone cut open the submarine? Why was there no urgency in the Admiralty's rescue system? Did the Admiralty really regret?

ISBN 0 9521020 8 0   £9.50 + £1.50 p&p

HMS THETIS – Secrets and Scandal – aftermath of a disaster.
by David Roberts

The sinking of *Thetis* cost 99 men their lives and is still today the worst submarine disaster in British History. This new book contains interviews with relatives of victims; sons, daughters, brothers, sisters and those very rare ladies, living widows. Also here are never before seen documents from the time; Offers of outside help, Secret Navy reports and even descriptions of bodies for identification. Why did the Official Inquiry blame nobody, explaining it away as 'an unfortunate sequence of events'? Why did the civil action on behalf of the widow's fail? Did the Admiralty cover it up? How much did Churchill know? How were those left behind treated? A huge publicly subscribed disaster fund was collected for the relatives. How was this managed and distributed? Who got what and why? What ever happened to the money that was left?

'a book that shocks...tells the hidden story of those left behind'   - Sea Breezes.

ISBN 0 9521020 0 5   £8.99 + £1.50 p&p

LUSITANIA by Colin Simpson - updated Merseyside Edition
THE definitive work on the real story surrounding this still mysterious ship.
On the 7th of May 1915 the Cunard vessel Lusitania was torpedoed by a German
submarine off the Old Head of Kinsale on the south west coast of Ireland resulting
in the loss of the vessel itself and 1,201 men, women and children. It also
ultimately resulted in the United States entry to the First World War. More than
eighty five years on the story of the *Lusitania* continues to be shrouded in mystery
and suspicion. What was her real cargo? Why wasn't she protected? Why did she
sink so quickly? Containing rare photographs from Germany and elsewhere; it is
a truly intriguing and fascinating tale.
ISBN 0 95201020 6 4 £9.50 + £1.50 p&p
CAMMELL LAIRD - THE GOLDEN YEARS
by David Roberts. Foreword by Frank Field MP
Looks back at the world famous shipyard's history with particular focus upon the
1960s and 70s when Lairds were engaged in the building of Polaris Nuclear
submarines. A unique look at the history of this yard that contains many
photographs and references.
'Captures life in the prosperous years of the historic Birkenhead shipyard'-
Liverpool Echo
*'Puts into perspective...the strikes...the Polaris contract...and those who
worked at the yard'* -Sea Breezes
ISBN 09521020 2 1   £5.99 + £1.00 p&p
LIFE AT LAIRDS - MEMORIES OF WORKING SHIPYARD MEN
by David Roberts
*When Cammell Lairds has gone and we are a generation or two down the line
who will answer the questions 'What did they do there?' 'What was it like?'
This book answers the questions.* - Sea Breezes
A Piece of Social History – Liverpool Echo
Life at Lairds is a book of more than 120 pages about what life was like for the
thousands of ordinary people that worked in the world famous Birkenhead
shipyard. Contains many rare photographs of Lairds, its' ships and its'
surroundings. ISBN 0 9521020 1 3 £6.99 + £1.50 p&p
A WELCOME IN THE HILLSIDES?
- The Merseyside & North Wales Experience of Evacuation 1939-1945
by Jill Wallis
A book that is both informative and moving, with the stories of the thousands of
children who left the dangers of Merseyside for the safety of North Wales
during World War II. ISBN 1 9029640 13 6   £9.95 + £2.00 p&p

115

FASTER THAN THE WIND - A HISTORY GUIDE TO THE LIVERPOOL TO HOLYHEAD TELEGRAPH. by Frank Large
Take a journey along the one of most spectacular coastlines in Britain, the beautiful hills and countryside of North Wales and Wirral. On a clear day it is possible to see just how signals were sent along the coast to and from Liverpool. This book contains full details of the intriguing and little known sites of the substantial remains of the Liverpool to Holyhead Telegraph Stations. A second journey can then be taken into the fascinating workings of such a telegraph and those people involved in creating and using the signalling system and what life was really like living and working at the telegraph stations more than 100 years ago.
ISBN 09521020 9 9 £8.95 + £1.50 p&p

IRON CLIPPER – 'TAYLEUR' – THE WHITE STAR LINE'S 'FIRST TITANIC'
by H.F. Starkey
'Iron Clipper' is subtitled 'The First Titanic' for it tells the story of the first White Star liner to be lost on her maiden voyage. Built on the Upper Mersey at Warrington, the *'Tayleur'* tragedy of 1854 and the *'Titanic'* catastrophe of 1912 are disasters which have so much in common that the many coincidences make this factual book appear to be a work which is stranger than fiction.
ISBN 1 902964 00 4 £7.50+ £1.40 p&p

FROM BATTLEFIELD TO BLIGHTY
THE HISTORY OF FRODSHAM MILITARY HOSPITAL 1915-1919
by Arthur R Smith
The horrors of the first 'Great War' are well known, but the stories of those sent back from the 'Battlefield to Blighty' tend to be overlooked. This is the little known story of one of the largest auxiliary military hospitals in the country that was established at Frodsham in Cheshire during the First World War.
Not for these men the modern diagnosis of Post Traumatic Stress Disorder or Stress Counselling after their ordeal... simply the green fields and fresh air of Cheshire and lots of TLC.
Over the period of the hostilities more than 3,000 patients were cared for at Frodsham Auxiliary Military Hospital and using a recently discovered set of contemporary photographs, *'From Battlefield to Blighty'* tells the stories of the doctors, the nurses, the patients and the local people who were involved in the Auxiliary Military Hospital at Frodsham.
ISBN 1 902964 16 0 £7.99 +1.50 p&p

'LIVERPOOL'S LOST EMPRESS' - FORGOTTEN EMPRESS
- THE TRAGEDY OF THE *EMPRESS OF IRELAND* - by David Zeni
Tells the fascinating story of the Canadian Pacific Passenger liner *RMS Empress of Ireland*. On her way home to Liverpool from Canada, she was sunk in a collision on the St. Lawrence River. Two years after the *Titanic*, it was, in terms of passenger fatalities, an even greater tragedy. These two ships, along with the *Lusitania*, form a triumvirate of maritime tragedies, all within a three year period, that sent shock waves around the world.

Yet whilst *Titanic* and *Lusitania* seem to be almost household names, the disaster that befell the *Empress of Ireland* has until now always been shrouded in the cloak of history, as impenetrable as the fog that brought about her total loss, along with 1,012 lives, on 29th May 1914. With a chilling connection to the 'Crippen Murders' and containing never-before-published material, *Forgotten Empress* grips the reader in such a way it is hard to put aside... a thoroughly excellent book.

...dubbed 'The 'Forgotten Empress'...the second in a shocking trio of tragedies at sea...sandwiched in between the disasters of the Titanic *and the* Lusitania,
...it was a sudden death... that sent Liverpool into mourning...'
Liverpool Echo

' Zeni brings a fresh, moment by moment urgency to this real life tragic drama.'' Winnipeg Free Press
ISBN 1 902964 15 2 £10.50 + £2.00 p&p
LUSITANIA AND BEYOND - THE STORY OF CAPTAIN WILLIAM THOMAS TURNER
by Mitch Péeke & Kevin Walsh- Johnson. Illustrated by John Gray
There are many accounts of the great maritime disasters, but very few portraits of the people at the centre of these vast, tragic events. William Thomas Turner was captain of the RMS *Lusitania* when the giant liner was sunk by a German submarine attack in May 1915, with the loss of more than 1,200 passengers and crew. Turner survived, and this is his story.

A Merseyside man, he came from Victorian seafaring stock and his sole ambition was always to go to sea. Turner became the outstanding seaman of his time, who had learned his craft the hard way- by experience.

The loss of the *Lusitania*, bound for Liverpool from New York, shattered his world and over the years he has been accused of treachery, stubbornness, ignorance and much worse. This book gives the true, remarkable story of Captain William Thomas Turner, the last Master of the doomed *Lusitania*.

'...the Admiralty made 'thoroughly discreditable attempts to blame Turner for the loss'... 'clears Captain Turner's name once and for all'... Liverpool Echo
ISBN 0 902964 14 4 £7.99 + £1.25 p&p

117

THE GOLDEN WRECK - THE TRAGEDY OF THE ROYAL CHARTER
by ALEXANDER MCKEE

The effects great of the great hurricane of October 1859 were to shock the nation. 133 ships were sunk, 90 were badly damaged and almost 800 people lost their lives. More than half of those that perished were on one ship - The *Royal Charter*, when she was lost off Anglesey on her way home to Liverpool from the Australian Goldfields. News of the wreck soon spread and the *Royal Charter's* other cargo, gold, became the focus of people's attention. Was all of it ever recovered? If not where did it go? The *Royal Charter's* gold still has the power to attract the adventurous and this book also explores attempts at salvage and treasure hunting more than 140 years on.

£9.50 & 1.50 p&p ISBN 1 902964 0 20

SCHOONER PORT - TWO CENTURIES OF UPPER MERSEY SAIL
by H.F. Starkey

Schooner Port tells the story of the part Runcorn and navigation of the upper Mersey played in the Industrial Revolution and of the contribution of merchants, the shipbuilders, and the crews in making Britain 'The Workshop of the World'. Also recounted is something of the courage and tragedy, which was the lot of many flatmen and seamen who helped build British industry on the strength of the shipping fleet.

'Recognised as the only authoritative work on this particular subject '- Sea Breezes

'Packed with hard facts and illustrated with some rare old photographs, this rare book should command a wide readership'. - Liverpool Echo

ISBN 0 9521020 5 6   £8.95 + £1.50 p&p

JUST NUISANCE AB - HIS FULL STORY
by Terence Sisson

The amazing but true story of the only dog that was officially enlisted into British Royal Navy, a Great Dane whose name was Nuisance, his official rank and name was AB Just Nuisance. Famed for his preference for the company of navy ratings (he wasn't too keen on Officers) in and around the famous World War II naval base of Simonstown, South Africa, Nuisance helped many a sailor rejoin his ship after a night on the town.

Today his own statue overlooking the bay off the Cape of Good Hope commemorates AB Just Nuisance.

£7.50 & £1.20 p&p

ALL AT SEA - MEMORIES OF MARITIME MERSEYSIDE
Compiled by Ev Draper.
Foreword by BBC Radio Merseyside's Linda McDermott
Introduction by David Roberts - Maritime Historian

A new book in conjunction with BBC Radio Merseyside's programme of the same name brings the voices of Merseyside seafarers and their lives to the printed page. Here are the stories of brave men, now pensioners, who survived horrendous incidents in the last two wars; stories of luxury liners, from Captains to cabin crew, of young lads forging their identity cards to get away to sea, and of their first eye-opening voyages.
ALL at SEA brings back the sounds and the smells of the docks, which remain vivid in so many people's minds, of busy tugs up and down the river, of men lost at sea; of women serving their country in different ways, and of those who provided guiding lights home. But through all the stories, there's one shining thread, the pride of Merseysiders in their seagoing traditions.
If you want real stories of the sea, told from the heart, by real people about real times and places, then this is a book for you.
ISBN 1 902964 12 8
£5.99 + £1.25 p&p

UNION - CASTLE -THE FORGOTTEN NAVY- by Peter Abbott
The Union - Castle Shipping Company was rightly famed for the Mailships of the line such as the Pendennis Castle and the Windsor Castle but there is much more to Union-Castle than just these well-known liners.
'Union-Castle - the Forgotten Navy' features the Intermediate liners, The Royal East Africa Service, Round Africa vessels, coasters, general cargo ships and reefers. It also covers the Zulu War, Boer War, World War I and World War II.
Using records from company archives, contemporary South African newspapers, the author's own and others private collections of Union-Castle ephemera, this new book about 'the Forgotten Navy' brings the reader a significant amount of hitherto little known material about the ships, the people and the Union-Castle Company.
£10.00 inc p&p
ISBN 1 902964 21 7

VIDEOS

CAMMELL LAIRD - OLD SHIPS AND HARDSHIPS
- THE STORY OF A SHIPYARD.

After an extensive search for moving footage of this world famous shipyard at work a video of the history of this shipyard has at last been compiled. How Cammell Laird served the nation through two World Wars, building world famous vessels like the *Rodney, Hood, Mauritania, Ark Royal, Windsor Castle* and many more, up to the tragic day in 1993 when Lairds was shut down.

The story of the yard is also told through the voices of the men who worked at Lairds; Welders, cranedrivers, electricians and plumbers, they tell of the hardships of building ships in all weathers and the lighter moments that came from some of the 'characters' of the yard.

£14.99 including post and packaging in UK.

'ALL IN A DAY'S WORK.' VOLUMES I & II
– A LOOK AT WORKING LIVES ON THE RIVER MERSEY.

Just when you might have thought that the River Mersey was dead and buried the biggest surprise of all comes along. There is life in the old dog yet! The River Mersey is alive and well. Liverpool, Birkenhead, Tranmere, Eastham and Runcorn are still places that enjoy marine traffic and employ people working on the river. There are interviews with River Pilots, shipbuilders, shiprepairers, tugmen and dredgermen that show that the age-old crafts and seamanship itself are still as strong as they ever were. There is also archive footage of working life on the river. Features Rock Boats, Mersey Ferries, the Bunker boats & crews on the Mersey, the Vessel Tracking System for river traffic, new vessels on the river, lockmasters and much more.

£14.99 including post and packaging in UK.

All videos are available in international formats for £17.99 + P&P £3.50.

Please state country/ format required.

To Order Books or Videos Direct Contact:-

Avid Publications, Garth Boulevard, Hr. Bebington, Wirral, Merseyside UK. CH 63 5LS. Tel / Fax 0151 645 2047

Look at the books and videos via the internet on

http://www.avidpublications.co.uk   or

E-mail info@AvidPublications.co.uk